D1314216

A Carnival of Sports

**Other Books on Social History
by Bill Severn**

The Right to Privacy

The Right to Vote

*The Long and Short of It:
Five Thousand Years of Fun
and Fury Over Hair*

*Rope Roundup:
The Lore and Craft of Rope and Roping*

A Carnival

# of Sports

*Spectacles,
Stunts, Crazes,
and Unusual Sports Events*

by
BILL SEVERN

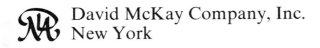 David McKay Company, Inc.
New York

ISBN: 0-679-20280-3

LIBRARY OF CONGRESS CATALOG CARD NUMBER: 73-92070

MANUFACTURED IN THE UNITED STATES OF AMERICA

Designed by C. R. Bloodgood

Contents

Introduction

Outside the main arena of major sports, beyond the TV horizon of baseball, football, basketball, and hockey, there is a great, continuous carnival of sporting fun. This book grew out of a desire to explore some of the sports fads of America, past and present. It is an attempt to capture in pictures and text some of that carnival—hopefully the best of it. But let no one imagine that this is the whole show.

Sports fads come and go. Some are temporary spectacles, stunts, and crazes; others grow into lasting sports or exciting annual events. A "sport," according to dictionary definition, is "something that is a source of pleasant diversion, a pleasing or amusing pastime or activity." And a "fad," Webster's says, is "a pursuit or interest followed usually widely but briefly and capriciously with exaggerated zeal and devotion." By those definitions, almost anything might be considered a sports fad. A complete account of all of them would be impossible.

So what is here is a selection, by author's choice and by no strict definition, of those fads, offbeat competitions, and unusual sports events that seemed to him the most interesting, most typical of their kind, or most fun to know more about. One small rule of thumb was adopted: They all involve some kind of physical activity, skill, strength, or endurance, and are not merely "freak" contests as such.

Thanks are in order, and are gratefully given, to the volunteer committee chairmen, chambers of commerce, Jaycees, and other groups that sponsor many of these events; to sports promoters, manufacturers of equipment, and all who took time from their own activities to help in the search for pictures and information. They took in a gawking visitor and showed him around the carnival, and helped him to discover the fun and excitement that made it a good trip most of the way.

B.S.

CHAPTER 1

Niagara Lookback

Niagara's
High Walkers

There were two great wonders of the world at Niagara Falls in 1859. One was the Falls; the other a thirty five-year-old French gymnast who called himself Blondin. He outdrew the Falls as a tourist attraction, brought the resort the biggest crowds in its history, and made himself world famous by walking a rope across the roaring waters. Blondin also started a sporting craze that sent a swarm of imitators, amateur and professional, scrambling over the ropes stretched between the United States and Canada.

Since his early boyhood in France, he had been demonstrating his athletic feats in high places. He had walked a rope across the Seine in Paris and the Thames in London, and had staged exhibitions in America for four years without gaining much fame or fortune. Blondin, whose real name was Jean Gravelet, had first come to Niagara Falls like other visiting tourists to see the majestic display of nature's power. When he announced that he intended to defy the rock-cliffed torrents by walking a rope across them, people called him crazy and started betting on how far he would get before he fell to his death.

He received financial backing and began to rig his gear for a crossing between Goat Island and the Canadian bank. Meanwhile, to stir up public interest, he took his daily exercise strolling up and down the high guy wires of an old railroad suspension bridge, casually puffing a cigar. His base was at White's Pleasure Grounds, midway between the Falls and Whirlpool Rapids.

Blondin, who started the craze for ropewalking across Niagara's waters, is pictured in his later years of fame and fortune, wearing some of his awards and royal medals of honor.

A small rope was first carried across the Gorge so the main cable could be worked into position. Wire-cored and covered with manila hemp, the thirteen hundred-foot cable, one and three-quarters inches in diameter, and costing $1,500, was to have a windlass at each end to draw it taut. Another 30,000 feet of rope were needed for guy lines. They were spaced about 20 feet apart to keep the cable from swaying from side to side, except for the long open stretch over the water where no guys could be fastened. The weight of the cable pulled it down at the center so that Blondin would have to descend a dip of some 50 feet and climb steeply again at the other end.

Long before he made his first walk, daily crowds gathered to watch the engineering feat of drawing the cable across. They got an unexpected show on June 23, 1859, when the small rope had pulled the cable to within a few hundred feet of the Canadian side. It stuck there and threatened to snap and drop the cable into the water. Blondin fastened a cord around his waist and daringly walked out on the small rope to hitch a rescuing line to the cable. News of his astonishing repair job out over the cliffs helped drum up an enormous crowd by June 30, the date set for his first crossing.

Hotels were packed with visitors, many of whom had traveled long distances to see him. Hundreds paid their way into White's Pleasure Grounds, and Blondin hired boys to take up a collection for him among the thousands more who jammed the riverbanks for a more distant view. Late in the afternoon Blondin warmed up by giving a special exhibition at White's. He danced along a rope and did somersaults, backward and forward leaps, and other stunts. But that was nothing new. Tightrope walking was standard fairground enter-

Taking time out halfway to Canada on one of his perilous walks, Blondin pauses for a midair rest and perhaps a casual snack from the pan balanced on his knee, during one of his stunts which included eating, drinking, and cooking omelets en route.

tainment. What the crowd had come to see and bet on was the sporting spectacle of his life-or-death walk across the Falls.

It wasn't until almost five in the evening when suspense had built to the breaking point, that Blondin started out on the cable from the American side. He walked it about a hundred feet and then sat on the cable and stretched out to lie on his back as if resting there nonchalantly. Every few hundred feet he repeated that until he had reached the middle of the river.

Far beneath him the little steamer *Maid of the Mist* came up the river. He dropped a cord to the deck and pulled up a bottle from which he took a long drink before leaping to his feet again without touching his hands to the cable. After eighteen minutes on the rope, he landed on the Canadian cliff. Half an hour later he walked back across the cable to the American side in seven minutes.

Blondin's feat made news around the world and made him an overnight sensation. Before a bigger crowd he made his second crossing July 4, this time with a sack over his head and body so that only his feet were free. Ten days later, when Blondin made a third try, the distinguished visitors who came to see him included former President Millard Fillmore.

To add still more to the danger of that walk, he risked being shot at with a pistol. Midway over the river he stopped and held out his hat, and from the deck of the *Maid of the Mist* below, a marksman named Captain Travis fired a shot through the brim of it. After finishing the walk to Canada, Blondin returned trundling a wheelbarrow over the rope in front of him. Early in August, before the year's largest crowd, he made the rope trip in less than six minutes, taking time out to stand on his head on the way.

In that age, long before television had made sports and show business full partners, Blondin managed to add some new crowd-thriller to each ropewalk attempt. On his fifth crossing he talked his manager, Harry Colcord, into sharing the danger with him by riding on his back. Colcord, who weighed 145 pounds, had a rough trip. One of the guy lines broke, and the main cable, pulled by the corresponding guy line, was jerked sideward. Blondin almost fell and was able to regain his balance only by running along the rope, "the impetus keeping us up," until they reached the next brace of guy lines twenty feet away. Colcord slid down off his back there, clung to him a few seconds, and then climbed aboard again. The trip took forty-five minutes and Colcord said afterward that "my heart was in my mouth all the way."

They discovered later that "unscrupulous and murderous gamblers" had tampered with the guy lines in "an attempt to kill us . . . trying to save their miserable stakes." The citizens of Niagara Falls awarded Blondin a gold medal "in appreciation of a feat never before attempted by man, but by him successfully performed on the 19th of August, 1859, that of carrying a man on his back over the Falls of Niagara."

Blondin offered to take other passengers pickaback over the rope for $25 a ride. It amused him to invite famous visitors to make the trip, especially when he was sure they would refuse. Among those who reportedly declined the invitation was the Prince of Wales, Britain's future King Edward VII. One man who did accept started shifting

Pickaback passenger: Blondin carries his one hundred forty-five-pound manager, Harry Colcord, across Niagara Gorge on his back. Later he offered to take others for twenty-five dollars a ride.

around dangerously on Blondin's back when they were out over the Falls. Blondin warned him: "Sir, I must request you to sit still or I will put you down right here."

He gave his first night performance with locomotive headlights placed at each end of the rope to illuminate it, and carried a pole with colored lights. When he was halfway across, the light gave out, leaving him in darkness. The only way those close to the cable could tell he was still safe was by feeling the vibration of his tread, until he finally appeared again before the cheering crowd at the other end. The next year he made the crossing on stilts forked at the ends to fit over the rope. He also walked backward, blindfolded, with his hands shackled, his feet in baskets, and performed such stunts as carrying a table and chair out over the water to sit on the rope while he cooked and ate an omelet or enjoyed a dinner topped off with cake and champagne.

On the strength of the fame gained in his years at the Falls, Blondin returned to Europe as the highest paid and most celebrated ropewalker in history. For another thirty years he made appearances around the world, winning medals and gifts from royalty, and built himself an impressive home called "Niagara House" in a London suburb where a street was named Niagara Avenue in his honor. There in semiretirement he still attracted newspaper publicity by the daily strolls he took at the age of seventy-two in the garden of his estate, not down among the flower beds but on a rope stretched high above.

Not everybody joined in praising Blondin. Some writers criticized his walks across the Falls as an "offense to morality" and said such sports belonged to "an age of savagery" and were a "disgrace to intelligence" on the brutal level of "the fight of a man with a wild beast."

That didn't discourage a host of imitators, although none of them achieved Blondin's lasting fame. Among the first of the rivals who appeared at the Falls late in 1860 was a Signor Farini, who put his rope across the Gorge near the hydraulic canal. Farini tried to outdo Blondin by having his feet bound in a loose sack. He also acted as a high-wire laundryman by collecting ladies' handkerchiefs which he washed while on his rope in a bucket of water drawn up from the river.

Perhaps the first American to cross the Rapids on a cable was Harry Leslie, who made repeated walks in 1865. The first woman to walk a rope over the Niagara Gorge was Maria Spelterina. She not only crossed in 1876 with baskets on her feet, but later walked with her ankles and wrists manacled. A man named Balleni embellished his walks across in 1873 by dropping from the cable into the river on a dangling rope.

Balleni had hired a Canadian house painter, Steve Peere, to help him erect his cable, and Peere decided one day to go across himself. He stepped out on the rope and made his amateur attempt, but Balleni was so jealously enraged that he tried to cut the cable with Peere still on it. Balleni was caught in the act, with the cable nearly severed so that a few more strokes would have sent Peere plunging to death. Warned in time, Peere scrambled back to safety. The bad publicity over such "unsportsmanlike" activity ended Balleni's career at Niagara Falls.

House painter Peere, made a hero by the incident, got some citizens to back him, and he later put his own cable across. Compared to the thick cables that Blondin, Balleni, and others had used, Peere's was a mere thread, only three quarters of an inch in diameter. He walked its hard and slippery surface successfully. But three days later he was found dead on the riverbank under the Canadian end of the cable. Nobody was certain what had happened, but the most likely explanation seemed to be that he had tried to walk the cable in the darkness at night without proper footgear or balancing equipment.

Peere's empty cable, still stretched across the Falls, seemed a challenge to other men. One, named DeLeon, aspiring to become Peere's successor, started across but became frightened after going a short distance. He slid down a guy rope, disappeared into the bushes, and was last seen scrambling up the bank on a ladder. Another amateur, Toronto photographer Samuel Dixon, was on his way to a con-

First woman to walk a rope over Niagara was Maria
Spelterina. To make it even harder for herself, she also
crossed with baskets on her feet, as shown in picture at left.
Like a tiny human fly high above the torrent, at right, Maria
kneels on her cable.

Another of the swarm of Niagara's High Walkers, Balleni, is
shown at left above the Falls and at right over the Rapids.
When amateur Steve Peere tried walking on the cable,
Balleni was so enraged he attempted to chop it down and
send Peere plunging into the water. Peere escaped, but the
incident ended Balleni's career at Niagara Falls.

House painter Steve Peere was an amateur who turned pro
after escaping Balleni's attempt to destroy him. On a cable of
his own, considered a "mere thread" compared to Balleni's,
Peere is shown at left crossing the Niagara Gorge and at right
balancing on a chair perched above the water.
Peere later fell to his death.

vention when he saw Peere's rope and boasted that he could cross it.
Nobody took him seriously until he made good the boast by walking
the same narrow path of steel. Dixon enjoyed the sport so much that
he later made numerous crossings and also learned to lie with his back
on the wire and pretend to take naps while balancing over the roaring
water.

Another Toronto man, Clifford Calverley, made crossings while
going through a gymnastic routine of walking part way on his hands.
I.F. Jenkins rode a bicycle on a rope across the Rapids, but it was a
specially built contraption with grooved wheels and balance weights.
George MacDonald frightened a gaping crowd by hanging head
downward by his feet from the rope he walked across. The craze of
ropewalking over Niagara Falls went on for some thirty years but was
never again the sensation that Blondin first made of it.

Another of the amateurs, Samuel Dixon, a
photographer by profession, enjoyed lying on his
back on Steve Peere's thin cable, as shown here,
close to the span of the suspension bridge most
people preferred to use for the crossing.

Leapers,
and Plungers,
Barrel Riders

Steve Brodie leaped to fame on July 23, 1886. Whether he really leaped on that day from the Brooklyn Bridge into New York's East River is less certain. He claimed that he did, and most of the world believed him. Brodie built a career on that claim at a time when a craze for plunging into dangerous waters had spread from Coney Island to the whirlpools of Niagara.

Brodie began life peddling newspapers on the Bowery, then Manhattan's amusement center and gathering place of the sporting gentry. The Bowery's theaters, saloons, and pleasure palaces spawned almost every variety of sporting event on which bets could be placed, from dogfights to pit battles between cat-sized fighting rats. Brodie, who had gained some attention as a high diver and swimmer, decided to put his name into the headlines of the newspapers he peddled.

The Brooklyn Bridge, itself a new wonder of the world, had lured several men before him to try leaping from its mighty span, not for suicidal self-destruction but as a sport that had the same result, since none of them survived. Much secrecy surrounded Brodie's own

Steve Brodie's leap from the Brooklyn Bridge on July 23,
1886, was vividly imagined for readers of *The National
Police Gazette* at the time. Although some doubted that the
Bowery newsboy ever made the jump, it brought him fame
and fortune during a sports-craze era of plunging into
dangerous waters.

"dreadful leap" on July 23. There were no witnesses who could later swear they had actually seen him walk out on the bridge. But there was a good crowd at the riverside. A body was seen to fall into the river with a great splash, and Brodie's head soon emerged from the water beneath the bridge. He was pulled aboard a rowboat, panting for breath but otherwise in fit condition to accept acclaim as "the man who took a chance."

Skeptics said it was all a carefully staged stunt and that Brodie never in his life "took a chance" on anything. According to the disbelievers, Brodie hid himself under a pier while a weighted dummy was toppled from the bridge to sink in the river, timing it to swim secretly underwater to where the dummy sank, so that he could come up a hero. But such rumors did nothing to diminish his immediate fame. Nobody was able to shake his story. He repeatedly refused large amounts of money to jump again from Brooklyn Bridge in the presence of chosen witnesses. "I've done it once," he said. "Once is enough."

For Brodie once was enough to make him a comparatively rich man and a celebrated public character. He capitalized on the publicity by appearing in variety halls and theaters and as the star of a road-touring melodrama plotted around the bridge-leaping feat. As the play's hero he had a fine curtain-closing scene in which he made a mock leap from a cardboard bridge as he cried out, "I'll jump and save the girl!" Eyes closed, he plunged a few feet to the stage amid a shower of confetti thrown up to imitate the spray of water, while sellout audiences roared approval.

Dark-haired, stocky, genial, he was a favorite of reporters, for whom he was always willing to stage publicity stunts. Some involved swimming and high-diving exploits, but from perches less dangerous than Brooklyn Bridge. He did risk real danger at least once more in his life. Seeking to add to his fame, Brodie traveled to Niagara Falls in 1889 and announced that he meant to swim the Rapids. By then Niagara's sporting athletes were gaining themselves worldwide notoriety for leaps, swims, and riding barrels in the roaring waters beneath the Falls.

According to published accounts, Brodie leaped into the churning riverflow from the Falls on September 7, 1889, protected by an India rubber suit heavily padded and braced with steel bands. Whether he really swam through the Rapids remained in question. Some eyewitnesses claimed that he did and that he was brought ashore bruised and nearly drowned; others insisted that he retreated from the icy water still clinging to a safety rope, afraid to let go. They claimed that he neither jumped nor risked a rope-free swim.

Brodie returned to the Bowery to accept plaudits for whatever it was he had done at Niagara Falls, continued his theatrical career, and prospered as the proprietor of a saloon where throngs of sightseers flocked to meet him in person. Many were surprised to find the ex-newsboy smartly dressed in expensive clothes, with big diamonds on his plump well-manicured fingers and more diamonds studded on his cravat and down the front of his fine white shirt. His fame gave him a lasting if uncomplimentary place as a word in Webster's dictionary where "brodie" remains defined as slang for a "suicidal leap" or a big blunder, fall, flop, or mistake.

Matthew Webb, left, famed English swimmer, lost his life trying to swim the Niagara Rapids in 1883, but three years later Boston policeman W.J. Kendall, right, made the swim.

In his lifetime, Steve Brodie did a lot better, financially at least, than most of the others who plunged into Niagara's waters. Many lost their shirts, and some lost their lives. Before Brodie's appearance at the Falls, an English endurance swimmer, Matthew Webb, was drowned in 1883 trying to swim the Rapids. In 1886 a burly Boston policeman, W.J. Kendall, impulsively tried the swim, protected only by a cork life preserver. He plunged in without advance publicity and had trouble afterward convincing anybody he had done it. The next year Alphonse King crossed the river well below the Falls on a "water bicycle," a foot-powered paddlewheel device supported by two air-tight cylinders.

A Philadelphia barrel maker, Carlisle Graham, started the craze for riding through the rush of waters in a barrel. He put a lot of work and much money into designing a series of big buoy-shaped casks and conducted trial runs of them filled with sandbags equal to his weight. Finally he produced a barrel in which he could stand upright inside a waterproofed canvas bag, holding two iron handles fixed to the inner sides.

Carlisle Graham's barrel plunges through the Niagara Rapids. Graham, a Philadelphia barrel maker, who started the craze in 1886, successfully rode in his barrel five times through the dangerous waters.

On July 11, 1886, Graham slid into the barrel, the lid was clamped on, and the strange craft was pushed adrift. It tumbled over and over, and inside the barrel Graham soon was sick to his stomach. Still he barreled his way through the whirlpool. Swept down the entire Gorge, five miles downriver in thirty-five minutes, he finally was fished out, boasting that he had "accomplished the impossible."

A month later Graham did it again, this time with his head protruding from the top of the barrel, so crowds ashore could have a full view of him all the way. He suffered a permanent hearing injury caused by the deafening slap of the water, but could hardly wait to get back into his barrel for a third and fourth trip that summer. Graham put his barrel through the whirlpool for the last time in 1901. The final

15

try almost took his life. Caught in the currents, the barrel whirled in mad circles for so long that he nearly suffocated inside it before he was rescued.

Meanwhile, not to be outdone by Graham, two barrel makers from Buffalo, George Hazlett and William Potts, built a two-passenger barrel and successfully went through the Rapids in it together in August 1886. That fall Hazlett took Sadie Allen along with him in the barrel instead of Potts, and she became the first woman to barrel-shoot Niagara's Rapids.

George Hazlett and Sadie Allen are shown with the two-passenger barrel in which they went through the Rapids together. Miss Allen, holding the lid that sealed them into the casklike craft, was the first of the barrel-riding women who soon outdid the men in dangerous stunting in Niagara's waters. Hazlett previously had made the run with a male companion, fellow Buffalo barrel maker William Potts.

Scorning barrels, Charles Percy made three trips through the Rapids in 1887 in a small boatlike craft, inside a covered chamber to shield him from the roaring water. He was challenged to a whirlpool race by Robert Flack of Syracuse, who appeared with a mystery boat called the *Phantom*. Flack claimed his *Phantom* was supported by an interior filling that he expected to patent for use in lifeboats, but he refused to reveal its secret ingredients. The race never came off, because Flack decided in July 1888 to test the craft before the race.

Harnessed inside the boat, he rowed it into the Rapids, and it immediately capsized. It was flung bottom side up with Flack trapped beneath it, where he died. The *Phantom*'s "secret" filling later turned out to be straw and wood shavings.

The following year Walter Campbell launched a flat-bottomed boat above the Rapids. With a pet black dog as his companion, Campbell stood up in the boat and boldly paddled out toward the seething pool. Luckily perhaps, his boat capsized before he reached the roughest water. With a lifesaver around his waist, he managed to

First woman to barrel-shoot the Niagara Rapids alone, Martha Wagenführer, shown with the barrel in which she survived being trapped for more than an hour before it was recaptured from the whirling current.

struggle ashore, but the dog was lost. That and several other misadventures more or less quieted the craze for a decade, but then the barrel riders came back with women in the lead.

Martha Wagenführer, the wife of a professional wrestler, was the first woman to try barreling the Rapids alone. Set adrift in her barrel the evening of September 6, 1901, she was whirled around for more than an hour before the barrel could be recaptured. She made it but was semiconscious by the time the head of the barrel was broken open to drag her out. Another woman, Maud Willard, who tried it at almost the same time, died in the attempt. Trapped inside a barrel for six

The woman who conquered Niagara Falls: Anna Taylor, an adventurous
middle-aged schoolteacher, plunged in a barrel *over* the Falls, not merely
through the Rapids beneath, and lived to tell about it. Top, she is put into
barrel above the Falls; lower left, she is helped ashore from the rock on which
it finally grounded; right, with the barrel afterward.

hours by currents that held it beyond the reach of rescuers, she was suffocated.

When Anna Taylor announced, that same year of 1901, that she meant to do what nobody had ever done by riding in a barrel *over* Niagara Falls, few believed her. All the previous barrel riding had been in waters beneath the Falls. Many headline seekers had talked of leaping the Falls, but no human actually had gone over, deliberately or accidentally, and lived.

Mrs. Taylor was an adventurous forty-three-year-old widowed schoolteacher. The barrel she had made for her was 4½ feet high, 3 feet in diameter, cushioned inside, and equipped with a leather harness and arm straps. To keep it upright, it was weighted at the bottom with a hundred-pound blacksmith's anvil. Air was supplied through a rubber tube connected to a small opening near the lid.

Some admired her courage, others called her a fool, but people came out by the thousands to see what would happen. Twice she disappointed the crowds and postponed the try because of high winds and poor currents. But on October 24, 1901, she began her voyage at Port Day, nearly a mile above the brink of Horseshoe Falls. From there she and the barrel were taken to Grass Island. She was strapped inside, the cover was fastened, and the barrel pumped full of air. Towed far out into the current, it was set adrift, the line cut at 4:05 P.M.

Tumbling, rolling, at times underwater, the barrel with Mrs Taylor inside cleared rocks and reefs that might have imprisoned it. Caught in the suction of the Falls, it hung a moment at the brink, then dropped on the long plunge into the foam-lashed river below. The barrel went over, bottom down, at 4:23, and a minute later shot to the surface. Swept downstream, it was caught in an eddy on the Canadian side, finally captured at 4:40, and grounded on a rock out in the river. Several men got the hatch off, and Anna Taylor lifted one hand out to wave, but before she could be fully removed, part of the barrel top had to be sawed away.

She was suffering from pains in her shoulders and back, a three-inch cut in her scalp, and she admitted that she had lost consciousness for a time during the plunge. Her first words when she recovered enough to talk to reporters were to warn others not to attempt "the foolish thing I have done." But Niagara Falls had been conquered, and by a woman, and after that there wasn't a lot left for other barrel riders to try.

CHAPTER **2**

Foot Spectacles

The Great
Pedestrians

America's number one pedestrian, Edward Payson Weston, walked his way to fame and fortune in the late 1860s and infected the sports world with a "walking fever" that raged for half a century. Largely because of Weston, walking contests for a time rivaled prize fighting and horse racing as an early big-money pro sport.

Foot racing had been common at country fairs before Weston was born in 1839, and distance walkers were setting records before he took up the sport at the age of eighteen. But Weston's endurance feats on the open road and at tracks and sports arenas spawned the publicity that attracted huge crowds of fans, filled the pages of sporting journals, fattened the purses of promoters, and turned pedestrianism into an international craze.

Weston first gained attention at the age of twenty-two when he carried out an election bet to walk the 478 miles from Boston to Washington in ten consecutive days to attend Lincoln's inauguration as President. He started from Boston's State House on February 22, 1861, followed by a swarm of fans riding in horse-drawn buggies, and walked the first five miles in 47 minutes before settling down to a steadier pace.

It was an antic that drew crowds to cheer him town by town, and reporters covered every mile of his marathon. A snowstorm slowed him some, and he slipped and fell several times, but plodded on through New England and got as far as New York the morning of February 27. Most of the time he ate as he walked, although he did manage to sit down to one solid meal each day. Sleep was in catnaps by the roadside or in farmhouse kitchens, and he began each new walking day at midnight.

The first of The Great Pedestrians, Edward Payson Weston, who popularized the international sports craze for distance walking contests, is pictured in a London sporting journal in 1876 at the start of his eight years of fleet-heeled success in Europe.

By the time he reached Philadephia, he was ahead of schedule, so he bedded down for a day in a hotel room. Weston then walked all night from Philadelphia to Baltimore, had breakfast, and started out in pouring rain to hike the final lap over muddy roads. He made it to Washington at 5 P.M. on March 4, 1861, too late to see Lincoln sworn in as President but still in time to enjoy dancing at the Inaugural Ball that night.

According to the terms of the wager, he collected only a bag of peanuts for his long walk. But he also collected reams of publicity and decided to turn professional and never to walk for peanuts again. He got his first big fee as a pro, and also created an international sensation, by walking from Portland, Maine, to Chicago in 1867 for a prize of $10,000. To win he had to cover the distance of more than 1,200 miles within a month, not including Sundays, which were eliminated to prevent a public outcry against sporting on the Sabbath.

Nattily dressed in a short jacket, a silver-initialed colored belt, tight-fitting knee breeches, a silk derby, and buff gloves, and wearing red-topped brogans, he took off from Maine on October 29 and covered the distance in 26 walking days, with enough time to spare not only to attend church services but to make speeches to crowds of admirers along the way. Weston carried a walking stick to chase away hostile dogs, but at one point he had to use his fists to beat off a man who attacked him in an attempt to halt the contest. He received threatening letters from gamblers who had bet against him, two attempts were made to poison his food, and he was warned that the only way he would reach Chicago would be "in a coffin." But he arrived the morning of Thanksgiving Day, his small feet hardly swollen, and was still fit enough to address a cheering crowd at the Crosby Opera House that evening on the benefits of walking as an outdoor exercise.

"The popular interest in this exploit, and the outpourings of people which greeted him from point to point on his journey, have made this feat one of the athletic events of the age," the editors of *Beadle's Dime Hand-Book of Pedestrianism* declared as they rushed that first of many manuals on the sport into print. "Such a task as his would have killed the most powerful horse, while the man has thrived under the operation, Weston having gained two pounds since he left home. He has achieved what no man ever attempted before."

For most of his long life Weston crisscrossed the country's roads on endurance walks against time for fat wagers and big prizes. He also competed against hundreds of other pros in walking contests at race courses and indoor tracks, where he drew such crowds that he was often paid three-fourths of the gate receipts. Some walkers beat him on level tracks in six-day matches, but few equaled his remarkable feats on the rough open roads.

He staged an endurance contest walking through snow in New England in 1869, covering 1,058 miles in 30 days. At St. Louis in 1871, he walked part of 200 miles backward and still covered the distance in 41 hours. In 1874 at Newark, New Jersey, he footed 500 miles in just under 6 days after doing the first 115 miles of it in 24 hours.

Weston went to Europe in 1876 to cash in on his international fame and spent eight triumphal and profitable years there in crowd-drawing exhibitions, mainly in England. In London in 1879 he won the Astley Belt, emblematic of world supremacy, by defeating British champion "Blower" Brown in a six-day "go as you please" match that allowed both jogging and heel-and-toe walking. He covered 550 miles in 141 hours 44 minutes.

At the age of sixty-eight in 1907, after constant years of grueling competition, Weston repeated the walk he had made forty years before, from Portland, Maine, to Chicago. He walked 1,345 miles in 24 days 19 hours to beat his own early record by some 29 hours. He celebrated his seventieth birthday two years later with the longest endurance walk of his life, across the United States from New York to San Francisco.

Weston started from New York March 15, 1909, hopeful that he could cross the country on foot by "a rather devious route" that would let him cover more than 4,000 miles in 100 days. By then there was a motorcar instead of a horse-drawn carriage to transport the judges and supplies. But Weston disdainfully rejected most of the "modern"

All but engulfed by a mob of admiring fans, Weston is shown in this newspaper sketch finishing the final lap of a four hundred fifty-mile endurance walk in England, while police hold back the crowd.

comforts offered him along the way and also held to his own ideas as to what was a proper diet.

He began his days at 3:30 each morning with a breakfast of oatmeal and milk, two slices of buttered toast, three poached eggs, three cups of coffee, a bowl of strawberries, two oranges, and half a dozen griddle cakes. On the road during the day he consumed eighteen eggs, each beaten up in a pint of milk with a tablespoon of sugar. "If I want a piece of pie while I'm on a walk, I'll eat it, or griddle cakes or pudding," he said. "The stomachs that can't digest ordinary food are those that are spoiled by high living or no exercise."

En route, at Kansas City, a whole club of women joined him for thirteen miles of his long walk and Weston used the occasion to urge all Americans to do more walking. "The average woman in England," he commented, "walks far better than the average man in America." But his ambition to do 4000 miles in 100 days was thwarted. For 30 days he was hit by heavy snowstorms and blizzards coming out of the West against him. He finally settled for a route that brought him to San Francisco in 3,795 miles, which took 104 days 7 hours. Undaunted, he turned around and walked back across the country the following year, from Los Angeles to New York, over a different route, covering some 3,600 miles in the record time of 76 days 23 hours.

Weston was still at it in 1914, at the age of seventy-four, when he tramped 1,546 miles from New York to Minneapolis in 51 days. Even after that he walked in some contests and exhibitions, but devoted more of his time to encouraging others to walk for health, competition, and the "joy of discovering the open road," warning that motorcars were making people more indolent than ever.

Ironically, the first great pedestrian was hit by a car while he was walking on a street in Brooklyn, New York, in 1927. He suffered injuries that kept him in a wheelchair most of the last two years of his life, and he died in 1929 at the age of ninety.

Weston's greatest rival during the heyday of pedestrianism was Daniel O'Leary. Born on a farm in Ireland in 1844, O'Leary came to the United States at the age of nineteen, worked in lumberyards and in southern cottonfields and drifted to Chicago, where he was peddling books from door to door as a salesman when Weston's fame inspired him to enter walking contests.

In 1874 O'Leary hired a Chicago skating rink and established his reputation by first walking 100 miles around the track in 23 hours and then doing 200 miles in 37 hours. By the next year he had made a 500-mile track endurance walk in 6 days and issued a challenge to Weston. The champion accepted and they met at the Chicago rink in a

Daniel O'Leary was an Irish-born
Chicagoan who did his first
endurance walking as a door-to-door
salesman. Inspired by Weston,
O'Leary became his greatest rival for
pedestrian honors and a champion of
contests on indoor tracks. He is
shown here at Gilmore's Garden,
New York, in 1878, in a drawing in
Leslie's Illustrated Weekly.

six-day match in November 1875. O'Leary, to the great surprise of
gamblers who bet heavily against him, beat Weston by walking 501
miles in little more than 143 hours.

When Weston went to England, O'Leary followed him. Backed by
a promoter of American minstrel shows, O'Leary staged walking
exhibitions in Liverpool and other cities. In London he and Weston
met in several matches with divided honors. O'Leary was the first
winner of the Astley Belt in 1878. He brought it back to the United
States and defended it in contests until a British challenger beat him
early the next year at Gilmore's Gardens in New York. It was Weston
who recaptured the belt for the Americans, after O'Leary had helped
make it the symbol of pedestrian championship on both sides of the
Atlantic.

O'Leary later made a lot of money exhibiting his walking prowess
in France, and in Australia as well as England and the United States.
By then American sporting journals were sponsoring all sorts of
"championship" belts for various walking events. One was known as
the O'Leary Belt. But there was much argument among judges over
what was a walk and what was a run, and great confusion over who
held what records. Most of O'Leary's fame came from track endurance
matches rather than Weston's sort of open-road walking.

John Hughes, another of the professional American heel-and-toers, walked his way to fame during the heyday of pedestrianism in the late 1800s. Hughes placed second to O'Leary in several important matches.

Possibly O'Leary's greatest performance was in 1907 at Cincinnati, where at the age of sixty-three he walked a mile at the beginning of each hour for one thousand consecutive hours. During the 42 days it took to complete the test, O'Leary's longest period of uninterrupted sleep was 50 minutes. The feat attracted the attention of the medical profession, and teams of doctors kept a record of his condition at the end of each mile. The terms of the contest were that if O'Leary broke under the strain, he would collect nothing. But he lasted it out and pocketed $5,000.

High society turned out in smart attire to help swell the popularity and gate receipts in the days when pedestrianism was a big-time pro sport considered somewhat more genteel than events such as prize fighting. View of the rather ornate walking track was sketched of a championship distance walk in a New York arena in 1869.

Astley Belt competition at Madison Square Garden in 1879, as pictured in *The National Police Gazette*, put thirteen top contenders into one of the series of distance walking races held on both sides of the Atlantic for world pedestrian championship. First won by O'Leary for the United States, the Astley Belt was recaptured by English pedestrian champ Rowell, then won for America again by Weston.

At about the time Weston was walking back from California to New York in 1910, another long-distance pedestrian, John Ennis, was crossing the country from New York to San Francisco. Ennis added a showmanly flair by taking time out for exhibition swims along the way. After a plunge into the Atlantic Ocean at a Coney Island amusement park, Ennis started walking on May 23, 1910. He swam in Lake Erie and later swam the Mississippi on a day he had walked 45 miles. As he made his westward way over the roads, he swam seven other rivers and lakes before reaching the Pacific at San Francisco on August 24. His total cross-country walking time was 80 days 5 hours.

A group known as "The Kansas City Hikers" made pedestrianism a family affair in 1913. Mr. and Mrs. Morris Paul teamed up with Mr. and Mrs. Gus Kuhn and their five-year-old daughter Ruth to walk for "health, pleasure and money" from Kansas City, Missouri, to San Francisco. They took their time, stopping for as long as five days at some places, and spent a total of 227 days in actually walking the 2,384 miles.

Professional walking contests continued through the years. Individuals continued setting records for walking stunts of one kind or another around the world, and walking competitions also became a recognized amateur sport. But sports fans discovered other events that were more exciting to watch. As the gate receipts dwindled and big prize money faded, the "walking fever" inspired by Edward Payson Weston and the other first great pedestrians lost its lure as a major spectator sport.

Start of the longest mass marathon in modern history
at Ascot Speedway, Los Angeles, March 4, 1928. One
hundred ninety-nine runners begin transcontinental
race with 3,422 miles to go in the carnival of mishaps
called "The Bunion Derby." Seventy-six of them quit
after the first sixteen miles, and only about one-
fourth of the starters made it all the way to New
York's Madison Square Garden.

United Press International

The
Bunion
Derby

In midafternoon of March 4, 1928, on the mud-soaked turf of the Ascot Speedway in Los Angeles, 199 men toed the mark for the first stretch of the longest mass marathon in modern history. Famed footballer Red Grange gave the signal, the starter's gun barked, and the legion of transcontinental runners took off on a 3,422-mile race for Madison Square Garden in New York and $48,500 in cash prizes.

Promoted as a "titanic struggle between the greatest long-distance runners of the entire world," it quickly became a touring carnival of mishaps, financial woes, blistered feet, and fallen arches, which caustic sportswriters dubbed "The Bunion Derby."

Few sports events had ever drawn a stranger entry list. There were half a dozen internationally known athletes among the racers, including several former Olympic runners and European distance champions, but for the most part they were homegrown unknowns of all kinds, ages, and conditions. Attired in a colorful assortment of track suits, determined old men jogged alongside youngsters in their teens, all hopeful of finishing in the big money. Each day there would be a race against time as well as distance, with each daily lap timed, so that the runner who won the most laps in the least total time for the whole distance to New York would be the final winner.

The racers' main qualification had been putting up an entry fee of $100 each, although a three-week training grind had cut the original list of 275 hopefuls to the starting band of 199. All who lasted out the full distance across the country were promised their money back, even if they weren't among the first ten who would share the prizes topped by $25,000 to the winner. But the man who expected to make the most out of the transcontinental race was its promoter, Charles C. Pyle.

Pyle was a Barnum of sports promoters, a Methodist minister's son who had dabbled in minor sports and theatrical enterprises before coming to prominence as the man who persuaded the fabulous Red Grange to quit the University of Illinois and play football for money. As Grange's manager, Pyle had promoted the gridiron hero into a million dollars' worth of contracts and product endorsements, taking a good share for himself. He had also talked France's Suzanne Lenglen and America's Vincent Richards into abandoning their amateur standing to star in cross-country tennis tours he promoted.

A glib talker and elegant dresser who often sported a derby and pearl-buttoned spats, Pyle was wise to the ways of extracting every possible dollar from such events. His initials, C.C., had earned him the nickname "Cash and Carry." As he saw it, the great transcontinental marathon would offer golden possibilities for everyone.

To start with, there were the entry fees collected in advance from the runners, which meant he wouldn't have to dip into his own purse to get the show on the road. Then there were the endorsements and commercial tie-ins for shoes, foot powders, linament, and sunburn lotion. He hoped to sell millions of official programs and the advertising space in them, and to profit from local concessions as his thundering herd made its historic way across the nation's hinterland.

His runners would pass through hundreds of towns and cities, hopefully drawing great crowds to watch the spectacle, which would mean booming business for hotels, restaurants, and stores. For the advantage of having his race mapped to go through one town instead of another, chambers of commerce and civic groups were asked to pledge promotional fees, to stage special store bargain-day sales, and to plaster their towns with his banners and posters. Pyle also expected to collect a fee of some $60,000 from the U.S. No. 66 Highway Association for steering his marathon along that route. In each town he would stage a traveling roadshow of vaudeville and circus acts featuring dancers, fire-eaters, trained animals, and sideshow exhibits, for

34

which he expected the locals to plunk down their money at his ticket booths.

Pyle traveled ahead of his runners in an advance motor caravan aboard a specially designed $25,000 "land yacht" called *The America*. In that age before elaborate mobile homes were common, the showy bus was a spectacle in itself, with deluxe sleeping compartments, a

Promoter Charles C. ("Cash and Carry") Pyle made a fortune promoting football great Red Grange and other sports stars and lost a good part of it when The Bunion Derby ran out of the money. Shown with megaphone giving instructions to the racers in what was promoted as a "titanic struggle between the greatest long-distance runners of the entire world"—and ended as what sportswriters called "the flop of the century."
United Press International

kitchen, two baths, and a so-called "radio information center" to keep the world informed about the race. Aboard it with him was his primary asset, Red Grange, to make personal appearances and join in the promotion.

Trouble began with the very first lap of only 16 miles to Puente, California. Unable to stand the foot-pounding pace over the hot highway, 76 of the 199 starters quit the race still some 3,406 miles short of their goal. As the runners reached the boiling flatland of the Mojave Desert a few days later, the heat, muscle injuries, and growing discouragement took their toll. One runner, struck by a hit-and-run motorist, brushed himself off and rejoined the race, but some of the others decided to give up the ground to the lizards and hitchhiked back to civilization.

Promoter Pyle had his own troubles with the care and feeding of his athletes, whose sweating endeavors produced such appetites that the outfit hired to provide for them demanded more money. Pyle broke the contract and fired the chef; the runners soon complained that they were getting nothing to eat but watery stew served on dirty plates. He finally farmed out the feeding to roadside stands along the way, allowing his contestants thirty-five-cent meals twice a day, which ended a threatened rebellion but not the grumbling.

They kept doing their assigned forty miles a day into Arizona, where Andrew Payne, a part-Cherokee farmboy from Claremore, Oklahoma, first briefly took the lead. When the troupe reached Albuquerque, New Mexico, the Chamber of Commerce decided it wasn't worth $5,000 to have them there and canceled the promotion. Pyle detoured his runners through the desert to avoid the town, but the same thing happened in other places, and his money problems grew into a tangle of broken contracts and lawsuits. The band of leg-weary marathoners failed to attract expected crowds, and even the traveling vaudeville show was a box-office bust.

Occasional rain and sleet washed the runners as they crossed New Mexico into the Texas Panhandle and footed it on into Oklahoma. Young Andy Payne again burst into the lead as they reached his native state, and local pride gave the enterprise a needed boost as people turned out to cheer the Oklahoman. Will Rogers joined in the celebration, and promoter Pyle made the most of the publicity that Payne was battling his way across the country in the hope of paying off the mortgage on his father's farm. He routed his runners through the state fairground, where the natives had to pay an admission fee for a good view of the marathoners in action.

But through Kansas, Missouri, and Illinois there were more disappointments and legal troubles. The crowds remained small, and the band of runners continued to dwindle. At the halfway mark and the end of the second month, the field had been reduced to some seventy who were still slogging it out. Red Grange quit the promotion in Chicago. The highway association, deciding that the marathon had strayed too often from Route 66, cut its payment to Pyle. There were rumors that his funds were running out faster than the race and that it might never get to New York.

He found new financing, and the survivors headed into the last

Andy Payne, nineteen-year-old Claremore, Oklahoma, farmboy, described as "part Cherokee and all heart," first took the lead in Arizona, reclaimed it again running across his native state, and kept out ahead through Pennsylvania and New Jersey to win the eighty-four-day transcontinental race in a running time of 573 hours, 4 minutes, 34 seconds. Shown here, he is still running strong, on last day's lap before finish in New York.

United Press International

thousand miles. Called "emaciated, unshaven, unshorn scarecrows," there were fifty-five of them still in the running in Ohio. Durable Andy Payne kept out ahead across Pennsylvania and New Jersey, and spread his lead to a comfortable 17 hours 28 minutes. Sportswriters were calling the great marathon "the flop of the century," but there was admiration for Payne, described as "part Cherokee and all heart."

On May 26 they began the last lap by dashing aboard a ferryboat that carried them across the Hudson and landed them in Manhattan, where a thin crowd of bored New Yorkers watched them foot their way up to Madison Square Garden. Four thousand spectators had paid their way into the 18,000-seat arena to see them complete ten turns around the board track, so that Payne officially could be declared the winner, after 84 days in which he covered the 3,422 miles in a running time of 573 hours, 4 minutes, 34 seconds. He beat second-place John Salo, a Passaic, New Jersey, shipyard worker, by some 15 hours.

But the award of prizes was put off for a week so promoter Pyle could make a special ceremony of it, with the hope that the second event would draw more paying fans to the Garden. Payne, the nine-teen-year-old winner, undoubtedly glad to get off his feet, was given an airplane ride to Washington the next day to visit the House of Representatives and hear himself praised from the floor by an Oklahoma congressman.

Survivors of the transcontinental race are aboard the ferryboat on which they crossed the Hudson from New Jersey to New York to end the 3,422-mile run with a final jog through the city streets to Madison Square Garden. Winner Andy Payne (number 43) is at extreme left.

United Press International

The forty-five runners who finished out of the money were paid back their $100 entry fees by Pyle, who admitted that he was deeply in the red, but declared that he was going to hold marathons all over the country and bigger annual transcontinental derbies each year. He also announced that his experience had taught him "more about toe trouble, heel trouble, instep trouble, and ankle trouble than any man living" and that he intended to write a handbook to sell, along with a new line of products to "treat anything that goes wrong from the knee down."

The grand finale at Madison Square Garden on June 1 disastrously drew the smallest attendance in the Garden's history, only about five hundred people, and many of those on free passes. Despite predictions that the winners would never get their prize money, Pyle kept his word and handed over the $48,500 in checks as a brass band blared, speeches were made, and newsreel cameras whirred. By then he had lost an estimated $150,000. "There has been a lot of talk about how much these boys suffered," he told reporters afterward. "But there is not one of them who suffered more than I did. My arms were sore all the time from digging down into my pockets and shelling out cash."

Convinced that he had learned what not to do from the mistakes of the first race, Pyle staged a repeat transcontinental derby in 1929, a reverse run from New York to Los Angeles. He found ninety-one starters willing to try, most of them veterans of the first disaster. The second runner the year before, John Salo, captured the $25,000 first prize for the 78-day jaunt, with a running time of 525 hours, 57 minutes, 20 seconds. Pyle wound up by losing another $100,000.

CHAPTER 3

Endurance Crazes

Pageants
of Fatigue

Dancing ability was the least of the talents of an assortment of athletic males and females, teamed as ninety-one couples, who lined up on the floor of Madison Square Garden on Sunday night June 10, 1928. Among them were eleven Bunion Derbyists who had run from Los Angeles to New York and several others who claimed distance running, walking, and swimming records.

Poised on their toes as three pistol shots were fired into the air at 9:57 P.M., they instantly moved forward when an orchestra broke into the strains of "Sweet Sue." What was advertised as "The Dance Derby of the Century" was under way. Marathon dancing, which had its start in honky-tonk endurance contests at the beginning of the 1920s, had been promoted into the realm of big-time sports spectacles.

Ever since the Twenties had emitted their first roar, there had been sporadic outbreaks across the country of dance marathons, nonstop dancing contests, and Charlestoners competing on highways and city streets. "Of all the crazy competitions ever invented," the New York *Evening World* had editorialized back in 1923, "the dancing marathon wins by a considerable margin of lunacy."

That same year Surgeon General Hugh Cumming of the U.S. Public Health Service had warned that excess marathon dancing might cripple hearts, wreck nervous systems, and lead to other afflictions. Cumming traced the craze to the dancing manias of the Middle Ages, when hordes of people feverishly danced in the streets for days until they dropped from exhaustion, driven by mass anxiety neurosis from such causes as the Black Plague.

But most of the marathon dancers of the Twenties seemed driven by far simpler motives. For the needy contestants there was the lure of prize dollars, extra pay for dance floor "sprints" of activity, side money from backers, gamblers, and fans. There was also ego-satisfying notoriety and the hope of being listed as better than also-rans in future record books.

Behind the 1928 event at the Garden was Milton D. Crandall, former press agent for Hollywood stars and stager of beauty contests. Inspired by the cross-country Bunion Derby promoted by his good friend C.C. Pyle, he decided to boost the marathon dance craze into the sports arena, hopeful that athletic footwork combined with a veneer of ballroom glamour would give him a box-office winner.

At the start on June 10, there was some semblance of orderly dancing, although the band was spelled between sets by a scratchy record player that ground out a ceaseless musical monotony. Potted palms had been spread across the Garden floor, and Crandall himself stepped out to join in the dance before a grandstand heaped with a citrus advertising display of lemons, oranges, and other thirst-quenching fruit. Surrounding concession booths advertised the wares of foot-ease peddlers and shoe and hosiery merchants.

Some male contestants were formally attired in tuxedoes, others in lavender blouses, silk shirts, white flannels. Their bobbed-haired partners wore short skirts, long skirts, evening dresses. One couple carried a black cat for a mascot. Another couple munched raw carrots for energy. Mary Promitis of Pittsburgh, whose dancing stamina soon won her the nickname "Hercules," revealed that she had soaked her feet in brine and vinegar for three weeks to toughen them the way barefisted prizefighters once pickled their hands.

Rules were simple: one hour of dancing followed by a fifteen-minute rest for sleeping, eating, and revival. A big wall clock marked off the hours, and the last team to survive was to collect a $5,000 prize. There were ninety-one red and white canvas booths around the arena, each with cot and chair, for the contestants and their trainers. At the end of each rest period, a tugboat-like horn hooted for the teams to line up and be checked.

Still alert and wide awake before the wearying hours of
fatigue took their toll, contestants are shown here soon after
the start of the endurance marathon in 1928 at Madison
Square Garden. As long as their feet were kept shuffling
while they enjoyed a snack from the refreshment table, it
was considered dancing within the rules of
the antic sports spectacle.
United Press International

Spotters walked the floor during the dancing to make sure contestants kept moving and didn't cheat by resting against posts and railings.
On hand were a judge, referees, timers, and a battalion of doctors,
nurses, masseurs, attendants. Female contestants able to stagger into a
beauty booth between rounds could get facials, manicures, and hair-
dos; a barber offered males free shaves and shampoos. Radio an-
nouncers broadcast hourly bulletins and floorside interviews,
cameramen almost outnumbered the contestants, and reporters for
the era's splashy tabloids turned the Derby into a headline carnival.

The first couple dropped out two-and-one-half hours after the
start. After two days and nights of dancing there were still sixty-six
couples two-stepping around on aching feet like mechanical toys
about to run down and badly in need of winding. Some snoozed while
dancing, with their heads on partners' shoulders, which was within

45

the rules as long as their feet kept moving. Tired faces and bandaged feet showed the strain, and quarrels broke out when one member of a team weakened while the other was still going strong.

Doctors advised a former Ziegfeld Follies showgirl to quit because her pulse was weak, but massage during a rest period revived her. Another girl injured her back when she slipped on a bar of soap taking a shower, but managed to limp into the lineup when the warning signal started the next hour. A sixty-five-year-old transcontinental runner, C.W. Hart of England, who claimed a record for previously outrunning two racehorses, was still prancing a lively foxtrot with his eighteen-year-old partner, but they didn't last much longer.

The New York Times wondered editorially "what kind of spectator might derive pleasure from the frowsy spectacle," and some prominent psychopathologists came to the Garden to have a closer look. But promoter Crandall was doing well drawing paying crowds of up to seven thousand. He admitted before it was over that he had grossed $121,000 but claimed that after expenses he would be lucky to keep $25,000. Visiting theatrical and political celebrities gave the Derby a box-office boost, making it the "in" place to go for New York's smart set. There was a nightly gathering of regulars who called themselves the "Goofy Club"—socialites, debutantes, men about town, leading columnists, sportswriters, Broadway and Park Avenue personalities.

Gambling was heavy. Although police were on the watch for bookmakers, with orders to run them out of the Garden, one couple was urged to stay in the contest for a promised share of a $3,500 bet. Another pair revealed that a $7,500 bet had been put on them. Published rumors had it that a total of $50,000 in bets had changed hands.

As the Derby plodded into its second week with twenty-eight couples left, nerves and tempers as well as feet began to fray. One man, kicked awake by his partner when he fell asleep in her arms, started dancing her around the floor with such fury that she passed out and had to be carried to her cot, putting them both out of the contest. Another man gave his partner permission to sock him on the jaw whenever he dozed. She socked too hard once too often, and he collapsed. Dancers exchanged kicks in the shins, slaps, stomped toes.

Some developed such fierce dislike for each other that guards had to be called to stop their assaults. Four men were needed to drag one fighting couple apart; a man was severely fingernail-clawed; a girl suffered a black eye. Others had hallucinations, like the girl who imagined she was a racing car that had trouble shifting gears, and the

46

man who chased an imaginary thief all the way down Eighth Avenue before recovering his senses and learning he had been disqualified for leaving the dance floor. After 206 hours of dancing, a girl was eliminated for screaming uncontrollably.

But most casualties were from plain exhaustion. Couples drooped, wilted, and dropped. Thirteen teams left at the start of the third week soon dwindled to nine. To make way for a previously

Dancing and dreaming was a fox-trot nightmare for some as they kept pushing aching feet around Madison Square Garden's wax-floored sports arena for four hundred eighty-one hours, even as they tried to sleep. Note the patches of adhesive tape at girl's heels to provide some protection against blisters. Barber's chair, left, was one of those used by males between rounds for free shaves and shampoos; there were also booths where the girls could revive sagging spirit and appearance with rest-period facials, manicures, and hairdos.
United Press International

scheduled boxing bout in the main arena, the Derby was shifted for one evening to the Garden's cellar, hot as a steam bath and smelling of animals recently stabled there by the circus. Moved back upstairs, it regained its nightly crowd of spectators. But some marathoners threatened to strike unless promised more money, and the rebellion spread to the trainers. Crandall settled those problems, but his troubles were growing.

One of the former Derby contestants, a young man who had quit after 257 hours and gone home to Wilkes-Barre, Pennsylvania, collapsed on a street corner there and was on the critical list at a hospital, hemorrhaging from a bleeding ulcer. Although there was dispute over whether the marathon was to blame, that was enough for New York City authorities. Goaded by mounting public protest, they had been looking for a chance to shut it down. Declaring the Derby "a public nuisance and a menace to health and safety," City Health Commissioner Louis Harris ordered it stopped at midnight June 30.

Crandall lost a court hearing to keep it going, and Commissioner Harris, backed by police, moved in on the Garden. After some squabbling and a threatened riot by pop bottle-tossing fans, Crandall accepted the verdict and seemed not too unhappy. He sweetened the purse, "to prove I'm no piker," by dividing some $8,500 instead of the promised prize of $5,000, splitting it eighteen ways among partners of the nine teams still on the floor. The big clock was stopped at 481 actual dancing hours.

As the 1928 Derby ground out its last minutes, the stands were jammed with spectators waiting for the clock to strike twelve. Some of the finalists broke into Charleston exhibitions, others sang or did cartwheels. Hannah Karpman said she felt as happy as a cat fed on catnip, and to prove it walked around the floor on her hands. When it was over, the cheering crowd made a rush to lift the dancers shoulder high. *The New York Times* called it "a fine funeral." Two of the couples finished out the night by making a round of Broadway cabarets—to go dancing. None of them got much rest because they were booked for a vaudeville tour that started the next day.

The Madison Square Garden contest generated publicity that spread the craze elsewhere. A theatrical weekly headlined the news that "Thirty Goofy Gallops" were under way in parts of the country, counting only those that were more or less major league at the time the Garden romp ended. Nobody knew how many smaller ones there were, but America seemed to be sprouting "corn and callous carnivals" as never before.

New York's Health Commissioner Harris put the couples dancing in another Harlem marathon under strict medical supervision. That event produced a dancing marriage. Without stopping their dance, a team of Harlem contestants from Chicago boarded a truck, and while two banjoists played for them, danced their way downtown to the Municipal Building for a marriage license, They danced back to the truck and two days later were still dancing when a minister performed the ceremony. But on July 4, with four teams left out of twenty-four that had started sixteen days before, Commissioner Harris finally shut down the Harlem contest.

When Newark, New Jersey, police ousted eighteen marathoning couples from a ballroom there, they boarded a bus and kept dancing

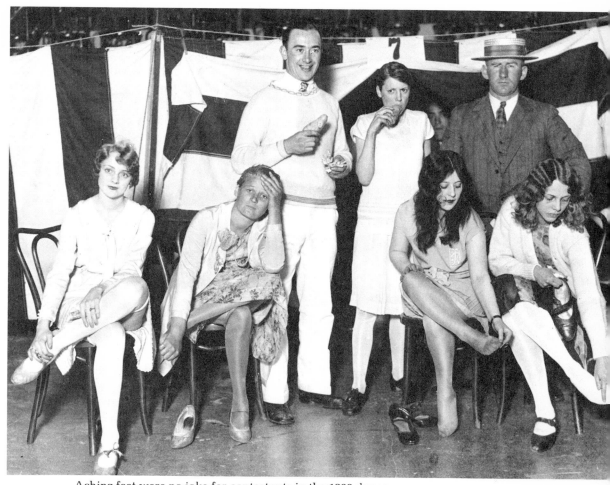

Aching feet were no joke for contestants in the 1928 dance marathon at Madison Square Garden, but they were always willing to put a best foot forward when posing for news photographers. Behind the group shown here is one of the canvas booths for the teams and their trainers, equipped with cots for sleep and revival during fifteen-minute rests after each hour of dancing.
United Press International

during a three-day odyssey over the Jersey hills in search of a new home. Rejected by several towns, they motored to the Bronx house of one of the contestants and continued dancing until promoters finally got them a hall on Broadway, where they were billed as "The Jumping Jersey Jiggers."

In Coney Island, at an outdoor marathon, dancers held out better than the spectators through hot sun and pouring rain. Sometimes there were less than a dozen ticket-buyers in the stands. After twenty-eight days of running into the red, with eleven teams remaining, the judges just faded away. There was no warning bell to alert contestants for the start of the next round. When they finally awoke from their cots, they discovered that the promoters and everybody else had disappeared along with the promised $5,000 prize. Even the press agent said he hadn't been paid.

Bunion Derby promoter Pyle, joining forces with marathon promoter Crandall, announced plans in August 1928 for a forthcoming "Transatlantic Dance Derby" via steamship from New York to Paris. It never came off, but as part of the promotion five of the finishing couples of the Madison Square Garden Derby danced their way over the Boston Post Road from New York to Bridgeport and back. As part of that event, cross-country runner Billy Busch ran backward from Bridgeport to Stamford. He footed the thirty-five miles in seven-and-one-half hours and claimed a new record for backward running.

Crandall did stage a second Dance Derby at Madison Square Garden in 1929. Rules were changed to appease city officials. Dancers got twenty-minute rest periods and two full hours off for showers and sleep each morning. The thirty-three starting couples included most of the stars of the previous Garden marathon and also a team of two Brooklyn girls dancing together. As added box-office attractions there were flagpole-sitting and rocking-chair endurance contests. But the second Derby failed to attract crowds, and Crandall shut it down on the twenty-second day with six couples still shuffling around to split $2,500 in prizes.

New York had become bored with the whole thing, although dance marathons flourished in other places well into the 1930s. Long before that Boston, Los Angeles, and many cities between acted to halt or restrict such contests, and some states took action. New York's Governor Lehman signed a bill in 1933 to outlaw any dance lasting more than eight consecutive hours. *The New York Times* was astonished that the law was still needed and asked: "Can it be that anything at all survives out of an age seemingly so very dead, the age of marathon dancers?"

Man at
the Top

"Shipwreck Kelly," who inspired men, women, and children to climb flagpoles and roost at the top of them, claimed at the height of his fame in 1930 that he had spent a total of 20,613 hours "in cloudland." Perched atop flagpoles on tall buildings in various cities he had endured 1,400 hours of rain and sleet, 210 hours in temperatures below freezing, 47 hours in snowstorms.

He went on climbing poles for another twenty years, and what he started never stopped. Ever since Kelly's time, although in dwindling numbers, others have sat on flagpoles in search of the publicity that once surrounded him as the self-described "luckiest fool alive."

Alvin Anthony Kelly, born in New York's tough "Hell's Kitchen" district in 1893 and orphaned by the death of both his parents, ran off to sea at the age of thirteen. He supposedly was called "Shipwreck" because of his boast that he had survived several ship sinkings during his years as a sailor, as well as two airplane accidents, three auto crashes, and a train wreck. But there were those who said his nickname came from his youthful career as a professional boxer, when opponents dropped him to the canvas so often that fans began chanting: "Sailor Kelly's been shipwrecked again!"

Knocked out of the ring, the banty five-foot seven-inch Irishman found work washing windows of high buildings, then got a job with a skyscraper construction crew walking steel girders. Discovering that he had no fear of high places, Kelly decided to become a professional stunt man. He balanced on rooftops, climbed walls as a "human fly," put on exhibitions as a high diver, and finally drifted to Hollywood, where he performed scripted stunts as a double for screen heroes.

In 1924 a Los Angeles theater owner hired him to sit on a flagpole atop the theater as a publicity stunt. Kelly stayed on the pole most of a day, drew a big crowd, pocketed a good fee, and at the age of thirty-one began a new career.

Americans in the Roaring Twenties turned out by the gawking thousands to stare up at what was then something new. "Shipwreck Kelly" on his flagpole, like a man pronged on the point of a giant toothpick, was a headline-making curiosity. Pictures of him captured such newspaper space for his sponsors that Kelly soon was earning a then hefty $100 a day. He was a one-man sporting spectacle, but not for long. Dozens of others got into the act, swarming up flagpoles from coast to coast.

Some of his many imitators borrowed not only the game but also his name, calling themselves "Shipwreck Kelly." He once counted seventeen other "Shipwrecks" in operation at the same time and had a few hauled into court in attempts to stop them, but finally gave up and just ignored them along with their claims that they could out-sit him. What annoyed him more than the competition was his complaint that their "unethical" methods were "hurting the profession."

Kelly took flagpoling seriously, with a Spartan-like attitude that shunned broad platforms, shelters, and other fancy comforts as beyond the realm of true sporting endeavor. His own endurance feats were of two kinds: sitting or standing. When he sat atop a pole for days, his perch was a small thirteen-inch wooden disc, the seat made of a metal brake drum from an old car, padded with just one cushion. He slept in five-minute catnaps with his thumbs locked into holes bored in the pole. Any wavering while he dozed would bring a sharp twinge of pain and alert him instantly so he wouldn't fall off.

When he stood, which was harder and more dangerous, it usually was only for hours instead of days, on an even smaller perch, a tiny six- to eight-inch platform. There were stirrups or rope slings to hold his legs, but no other support to keep him standing. Whether he was sitting or standing, although he could shift position and move

52

Alvin "Shipwreck" Kelly's flagpole feats inspired men,
women, and children to scramble up poles to perch at the
top. Star attraction at Madison Square Garden in 1929, he
stole the show from a dance marathon by standing pole-high
on an eight-foot platform, twenty-one hours a day for
twenty-two consecutive days.
United Press International

around a bit, Kelly's greatest problem was lack of exercise and the deadening of circulation in his legs. His food and other necessities were hauled up in a basket on a rope pulley, and the same rope was used to haul down a washbasin and pot that were also needed by a man stranded on a flagpole without bathroom facilities. A covering blanket, discreetly used, afforded privacy.

By 1927 the craze he started had so many rivals up on poles that police in Boston, Los Angeles, and several other cities moved to arrest them as public nuisances. Kelly himself later had some brushes with the law. New York police ordered him down from one pole over a midtown hotel because he was attracting crowds that choked Times Square traffic. Another time a zealous minion of the law forced Kelly down from his perch by threatening to chop the pole out from under him. But his prestige as the nation's number one flagpoler usually won municipal tolerance. Mayors and other officials were happy to pose for pictures with him and bask in his publicity.

At times he perched on poles aboard moving trucks and even atop planes flying through the air. Occasionally he stood on his head, pole-stunting upside down at least long enough to consume doughnuts, coffee, or some other product sponsors paid him to promote. In addition to collecting advertising fees, he usually was well paid by the owner of the site, shared in rooftop admission receipts, and had agents down on the street peddling pamphlets of his "life story."

Each year Kelly broke his own previous endurance records. Probably his best record for flagpole standing was made at Madison Square Garden in 1929. During his stand there reporters were hauled up by rope for flagpole-top interviews. Kelly had to compete with a dance marathon going on at the same time but he stole the show. He stood pole-high on an eight-inch platform twenty-one hours a day for twenty-two consecutive days.

The same year he set a then "world's record" for flagpole-sitting by staying aloft twenty-three days at a Baltimore amusement park. When he came down, the crowd-roaring acclaim made him such a hero to the young that the whole city blossomed out with juvenile pole-sitters. Boys and girls from the age of eight upward took to the tops of trees and backyard poles at such a rate that in a single week reporters counted twenty-five young disciples of "Shipwreck Kelly" at roost. As the epidemic spread, newspapers and national magazines sounded editorial alarm, and public moralists demanded a mobilization of parents to apply hairbrushes and straps to the posterior of pole-sitting young America. But for the most part the young pole-perchers were encouraged by adults eager to share their notoriety.

Avon "Azie" Foreman, a fifteen-year-old boy, started an outbreak of juvenile flagpole-sitting in 1929, when dozens of youngsters took to roosting in treetops and on backyard perches. Inspired by "Shipwreck Kelly," young Foreman sat on a pole behind his Baltimore home for more than ten days, attracted thousands of spectators, and even brought out the city's mayor to present him with an official scroll of honor. Before the epidemic ended, boys and girls from the age of eight were pole-sitting, city inspectors were working overtime issuing special licenses for the kids to perch, and the nation's press was in an editorial uproar.

United Press International

Baltimore's outbreak began when fifteen-year-old Avon "Azie" Foreman mounted a backyard pole topped by an old ironing board to sit there until he was recognized as "the champion juvenile flagpole sitter of the world." Nightly crowds grew until an estimated four thousand people came to see him on his makeshift platform, bathed in spotlights set up by his electrician father. When not sleeping or eating Avon sang snatches of a song called "The Flagpole Melody" and exchanged shouted conversations with a girl friend who kept vigil at the base of the pole.

Avon stayed up 10 days, 10 hours, 10 minutes, 10 seconds before descending amid a bedlam of cheers and honking auto horns. Mayor William Broening was there in person to present him with an autographed testimonial bearing the great seal of the City of Baltimore. The mayor made an address praising Avon for his "grit and stamina," reflective of "the pioneer spirit of early America" that was so essential "in the great struggle of life."

With that kind of encouragement Baltimore sprouted young pole-sitters everywhere. Avon soon lost his title to twelve-year-old Jimmy Jones, who stayed on his backyard perch an hour longer and dutifully practiced his violin lessons while in midair. Another boy the same age, William Wentworth, had the support of his church pastor, who led a preach-in and assembled the congregation for a hymn-sing around Billy's flagpole. Girls soon took to the sport, some hoisting chairs, mattresses, and other home comforts with them to their tent-sheltered platforms.

Parents of rival contenders feuded bitterly over what was honest pole-sitting and what was not. Mayor Broening impartially made the rounds, handing out autographs and words of praise. But after several youngsters toppled and hurt themselves, city officials tried to restrain the fever by issuing flagpole safety specifications and charging would-be sitters a one-dollar license fee. Police worked overtime checking riggings.

Neighborhood merchants rented pole space for tacking up advertising posters, and every juvenile pole site also had its collection box so spectators could deposit nickels and dimes. Some parents ran refreshment stands for the sale of popcorn and soft drinks. The *Literary Digest* editorially frowned, the *New Republic* wondered whether Baltimore's adults and not the young pole-sitters should be morally spanked, and *The New York Times* said "serious doubts of civic sanity are certainly warranted." But it wasn't until the end of summer and the opening of school that the last of "Shipwreck Kelly's" young imitators finally was brought to ground.

Kelly accomplished the greatest feat of his own pole-sitting career the next summer at Atlantic City. On June 21, 1930, he climbed atop a 125-foot mast above the New Jersey shore resort's Steel Pier, hoping to stay on his 13-inch perch long enough to beat his previous record of twenty-three days aloft. When he had smashed the record on July 14, he decided to stay up a little longer. He was gaining weight from inactivity, but cut down to one meal a day and hung on. Five days later Kelly was still there, and a doctor who was hoisted up the rope to examine him pronounced him in good condition.

He kept busy answering hundreds of fan mail letters basketed up to him, making nightly pole-top radio broadcasts, and sending messages down to the boardwalk crowds below to tell them how much he was enjoying the cool ocean breeze while they sweltered in the sun. There was more than a breeze at times; storm winds whipped and swayed his flagpole, and he endured thunderstorms and hail.

Finally, on August 9, he decided to come down and prepared himself to greet his public by first having a shave, haircut, and manicure. A girl *The New York Times* called "one of the prettiest of barberettes" was pulled up the rope to give him an hour's tonsorial overhauling. The "whopping cost of the treatment" was $4.25. Kelly grandly handed her a five and waved aside the change.

Twenty thousand cheering people were on hand when he made his slow descent that afternoon, and there was a flood of congratulatory telegrams from prominent Americans. Kelly had trouble using his feet when he first touched ground, but was able to shake hands with the official dignitaries who welcomed him back to earth and to pose for newsreel cameramen. By nightfall he had recovered sufficiently to make personal appearances at theaters before attending a grand reception and celebration in his honor at the Steel Pier.

He had been on his flagpole for 1,177 hours, more than forty-nine days, which was a record nobody broke for nearly another decade, discounting the claims of those who roosted on large platforms or in sheltered pole-top coops. Kelly himself never equaled it again. That December he made another try, 400 feet above the street on a pole over a newly opened Times Square hotel in New York, but he quit after thirteen days, beaten down by the bitterly cold weather and even more by the grip that the Depression had taken on American pocketbooks.

When he began that New York sit, Kelly announced that he meant to donate the proceeds from the sale of his "life story" pamphlet to the unemployment fund of the Disabled American War Veterans. His pole-sitting did provide an unexpected benefit for some of the

"Shipwreck Kelly," perched on pole high above the street,
tries for a new sitting record at Union City,
New Jersey, in 1929.
United Press International

unemployed. Forty men turned up in Times Square with telescopes and field glasses, which they rented out for a nickel a look to spectators who wanted to watch Kelly atop the pole.

But even they didn't do as much business as street-corner apple sellers. Kelly, heavily out of pocket for his own expenses, raised only thirteen dollars in thirteen days for the veterans' fund and came down from his frozen flagpole in disgust. "I thought I had a depression-proof business," he said, "but I was wrong. I wasn't making any money and I didn't seem to be doing anyone else any good."

He went on flag-poling through the Thirties and into the Forties, but his fame gradually faded as a new crop of pole-sitters came along. On October 11, 1952, Kelly collapsed on the sidewalk and died of a heart attack, not far from Madison Square Garden where his name once had been up in lights. Under his arm was a scrapbook of old news clippings from the days when he had been a headliner. In the nearby furnished room where he had been living on relief, police found a single duffel bag of personal belongings, mostly old ropes and flag-pole-sitting gear.

After him, even in the 1970s, there were others still claiming new records, some for perching on high for as long as eight months, but many of them did their sitting on broad platforms, in tents, huts, big plastic bubbles, and with all the conveniences of home, which "Shipwreck Kelly" would have called not flagpole-sitting at all. There being no rules, the standards of pole-top living varied so much nobody could really say what the record was.

When it came to that, way back in the Fifth Century a Syrian monk, St. Simeon Stylites, lived for thirty years as a religious hermit atop a sixty-foot pillar of stone. One of his followers, Daniel the Stylite of Constantinople, spent thirty-three years on one 66 feet high. But among moderns it all began with Kelly, and flagpole-sitting has never since had as big a star, or luckier fool. "I could have stayed up longer," he once said after a sitting. "But what would it prove? I was up there long enough."

CHAPTER 4

Rolling Along

Born in the dance marathons of the 1930s, turned from an
endurance contest into a sport that borrowed from football,
ice hockey, pro wrestling, and bike racing, Roller Derby was
reborn again in the Forties, Fifties, and Sixties, and has
rolled into its greatest popularity in the 1970s,
streamlined and highly portable.
Bay Promotions, Inc.

The
Indestructible
Roller Derby

That madness on skates, the Roller Derby, has rolled down the decades from the 1930s, alive and well and living in its own wonderland. As a package of sports action, freewheeling mayhem, and traveling circus, it has had more comebacks than a cat with nine lives. Every time it seemed about to die, a new generation of fans rediscovered the Derby and revived its popularity.

Roller Derby was a one-man invention. Leo Seltzer created it, named it, developed it, and nursed it through depression, war, and indifference to its first golden years. Seltzer, who got his start promoting epics of the silent screen, had become a theater owner in Portland, Oregon, by the time dance marathons hit there in 1929. When a marathon at a nearby amusement park started packing in more customers than his movie theater, he decided to cash in on the craze with a contest of his own.

Although there was no roller-skating involved in the first package he put together, it contained some of the basic ingredients of the success formula for later Roller Derbies. Since the weary couples who

shuffled around in dance marathons never really danced, he presented his version as a "walkathon." Couples plodded the floor in an
endless circling walk, with the added action of heel-and-toe races and
other side events. Seltzer gave his walkathon a small-town test run,
expanded it, and in 1930 invaded Denver, Colorado. Pushing that
combination of show biz and sports across the country, he promoted
walkathons for four years and made a good pile of money.

By then the walkathon had passed its peak, and he looked for
something new to promote. His thinking was triggered by a magazine
article that said roller-skating was the nation's unrecognized top sport
which nearly all Americans enjoyed at some time in their lives. He
himself had never tried on a pair of skates, but at a Chicago restaurant
one night he worked out his first plans for a skating contest, doodling
them in pencil on the tablecloth. On August 13, 1935, at the Chicago
Coliseum, he presented the world with what was billed as a "Transcontinental Roller Derby."

It was only a pale promise of Derbies to come, since it was largely
a walkathon on wheels that sent teams of men and women skaters
lapping around an oval wooden track in a test of endurance. Even so,
the novelty drew twenty thousand spectators to the Coliseum, and
Seltzer knew he had something. He also had problems with the track.
Skaters raced for speed along the straightaway, hit the shallow curves,
and went sailing off into the air to crash in the stands. With timbers
and screw jacks he banked the curves up to an angle that conquered
centrifugal force and padded the railing with rubber. There were still
a lot of bumps, bangs, and falls, but they soon became part of the
game.

Seltzer road-toured the Roller Derby to other cities and began to
rewrite the rules to change it from just an endurance race into more of
a sport of opposing teams and players. The biggest change came during a Derby contest at Miami, where writer Damon Runyon happened
to be watching when the skaters piled up in a bone-thudding tangle.
That was what the Derby needed, Runyon told Seltzer, body contact
to turn it into real sport. Seltzer opened the rules to add muscle to
speed, and the game gradually grew into a roller-skating combination
that borrowed from football, ice hockey, pro wrestling, and the lapping and jamming of bicycle races.

From the start, as a heritage of its walkathon beginnings, women
skaters were a big part of the Derby's appeal. Long before women's lib,
the Derby claimed to be the first professional sport in which women
competed equally with men under the same rules of play and with
scores equally combined for team totals. Each team came to have ten

Writer Damon Runyon helped turn Roller Derby into real sport in the early days by saying what it needed was body contact to add muscle to speed. Modern Derby pivots are shown battling here in football-like blocking action on wheels as Red Devil defenseman Bob Woodbury, left, confronts coach Bill Groll, right, of the Chiefs.
Bay Promotions, Inc.

players, a five-woman squad and a five-man squad, skating in alternate time periods against squads of an opposing team.

Play began with two opposing squads lined up in a pack. One or more members of a team then started a jam by sprinting away and circling once around the track to come up to the pack from behind and try to battle past enemy players. While teammates blocked and skated interference, the jammer tried to smash through or batter opponents out of his way. He scored one point, up to a total of three points, for each opponent he passed within a time limit.

The rolling battles of body slams, crack-the-whip speed plays, hip jolts, leg and shoulder thrusts—all designed to sprawl opponents on their backs or spin them against the rail—frequently erupted into kicking, slugging, wrestling brawls. For obvious foul play a skater could be sent to a penalty box, but since the paying customers came to see action, rules were not always strictly observed.

In the early days mixed teams were tried, but the public wouldn't accept direct physical warfare between the sexes, so that idea was abandoned and male and female squads were kept separate. But no

65

Roller Derby claims to be the first professional sport in which women have always competed equally with men, part of its appeal since the dance marathon era of the 1930s. This female whip-de-do is a standard play to whip the girl at the end of the chain toward a scoring point.
Jonathan Perry

such sentiment prevented fans from cheering the girls on to attack each other, and the female Derbyists proved at least as rough in battle as the males. Their feuds often were personal vendettas, carried on for months from game to game. Women fans also sometimes got into the fray by leaning over guardrails to whop at passing skaters with their pocketbooks or to whack at them with pop bottles. Excited male fans now and then leaped the rail to join in a brawl and land a haymaker on some player's jaw.

As in pro wrestling, some of the pain and rage of the game was staged hokum, but a lot of it was for real and so were accidents and fracturing injuries. Nearly all Derby players suffered broken bones and other body damage at times, but no more than players in other rough contact sports. They learned to take most blows and falls to avoid serious injury, and they also learned, as the game went along, to become more skilled in strategy and team play. Eventually each five-player squad had two designated jammers, two blockers, and a pivot player who could either block or jam.

After its first brief life as an endurance carnival, different from the faded dance marathons, the Derby began a second life as a sports spectacle that appealed to a new box-office generation of thrill-seekers in the early 1940s. Fans created their own stars, among the biggest of them a Chicago housewife, Mrs. Joseph Bogash, a woman in her forties when she applied to be taken on as a player because a

Rolling battles frequently erupt into wrestling brawls, some staged to entertain the paying customers, some real. Caught between in this female tussle, a male official tries to break it up.
Bay Promotions, Inc.

doctor had recommended roller-skating for exercise. Seltzer recognized her box-office potential and signed her up, along with her teen-aged son Billy who later was an outstanding Derby star himself. Mrs. Bogash became the Derby's most colorful early attraction as "Maw" Bogash, a formidable figure in helmet and padding who tipped the scales at 160 pounds and battled her way through games for fifteen years, outskating rivals half her age.

But after a decade of financial ups and downs, the Derby's popularity waned again. Seltzer had tied up a tight monopoly of franchises and arena contracts, but expenses were high and profits thin. In Chicago at the home-based Coliseum, the Derby still had devoted fans. On its road tours even cut-priced admissions failed to bring out the spectators. Generally ignored by newspapers, seldom mentioned by sportswriters who refused to accept it as a serious sport, it withered mainly because most of the public was unaware of what it was.

Seltzer revived it by turning to television, which itself was just catching on in a big way. He paid his own money to sponsor the first televised game on a Chicago station in 1947. Before it was over, the switchboard was jammed and a box-office rush followed. He brought the game into New York, and the first night's gate was only $500. But after it was seen on television, the next night was a sellout. Seltzer never again had to pay for TV showings; sponsors paid him. Roller

Roller Derby's highest-paid superstar, Charlie O'Connell
(number 40), veteran of more than twenty years of banked
track competition, is known to fans as "Mr. Roller Derby."
The six-foot two-inch biggest wheel of the sport is one of
only two active skaters in the Derby Hall of Fame.
Bay Promotions, Inc.

Derby was on its way toward becoming a television and box-office
sensation.

Thousands of Americans hunkered down happily in their living
rooms to watch as the Derby captured prime-time evening showings in
New York three nights a week and was relayed over the country via a
national TV hookup. Derby teams, multiplying to play in halls and
arenas across the United States, drew several million ticket buyers in
1949. By then the Derby was topping TV popularity ratings and had
become what *The New York Times* television columnist Jack Gould
called "an accepted way of life in pub and parlor," with viewers ready
to drop everything to watch. "The Derby's disruptive effect on the
household is virtually absolute," he wrote. "Never before has roller-
skating meant so much."

Derby stars vied for TV eminence with comedian Milton Berle
and in person were mobbed for autographs. Nightly watchers clung to
their sets to see if Midge "Toughie" Brashun would score a point,

break a leg, or win one of her celebrated hair-tugging battles. The first "World Series" of the National Roller Derby filled Madison Square Garden for a week in September 1949 with crowds of up to 13,000. By 1951, in the third straight year of series games at the Garden, the Derby was drawing a record attendance of nearly 19,000, with women a large part of its audience. Veteran sportswriters reported they had seldom seen such "wide-eyed enthusiasm" and "cultlike fanaticism" among fans. It was also reported that the sport was spreading to amateurs, with kids chalking Derby ovals on their playgrounds. Other promoters, cashing in on the craze, organized rival skate games under other names.

But in the mid-1950s television's glow began to burn out for the Derby. Having produced a golden egg, TV cooked its own goose with overexposure. Network moguls laid the sport to waste by overscreening games so often that the Derby became commonplace in home living rooms. Roller Derby 365 days a year, with hardly a commercial break between seasons, was too much; as ratings bottomed out sponsors deserted and box-office lines thinned.

The Derby vanished from Madison Square Garden and New York television in 1954, attempted two big-time New York comebacks later in the Fifties, and finally all but disappeared from the East. Retreating westward, it eventually established a new base in the San Francisco

The League's leading scorer, Mike Gammon, left, and one of the game's top defensive skaters, veteran pivot Ronnie Robinson, right, son of boxing's great Sugar Ray Robinson.
Bay Promotions, Inc.

Bay area. It never completely died, but except for loyal fans, few held out much hope for its national recovery.

Then in 1958 Leo Seltzer's son Jerry took over and slowly began to breathe life into the Derby once again. He repackaged Roller Derby's old values into a new product of sports excitement that could be taken on one-night stands to hundreds of towns major sports events seldom reached, and he learned to use television to exploit the Derby in all of those towns.

TV had come into a new technical age that could replace live shows with film and tape. Once filmed, the Derby games could be shown later, anyplace at any time. Jerry Seltzer produced the best of the Derby play on tape, big, fast-moving games with the best skaters the Derby had, and put them on living room screens for another TV generation. Then he brought the Derby's touring stars as close to every TV viewing home as he could. The result was a revolutionary success.

Everything at first centered around one team, the sensational San Francisco Bay Bombers. For twenty-one weeks a year, from April to September, the Bombers played home-area games against various visiting teams also all owned by Seltzer. At home they became the biggest professional sports attraction in the area, drawing a larger regular attendance than all other sports with the possible exception of baseball. They soon had an even greater audience across America. Videotape turned the Bay Bombers into the "home team" of some twenty million Roller Derby fans everywhere in the United States.

Sunday night Bomber games were taped, not for network TV but for later local screening by individual stations, to be shown at whatever time slots were convenient. Screened in some cities at odd daytime or early morning hours, they still attracted enthusiastic fans who seemed to care not at all that they were watching games played by the Bombers days or weeks before.

Derby tapes actually outpulled competing live pro football games in a few cities, maintained high ratings elsewhere, and attracted sponsors. But their main purpose was to promote excitement over the Roller Derby itself and make fans anxious to turn out to see the famous Bay Bombers on tour. Like movie trailers, the tapes built up the coming attraction, with constant announcements of upcoming live games in each TV area.

As soon as the home season ended, the Bombers took to the road, hopscotching thousands of miles up, down, and across the country for games in different places five nights a week, hitting every town where they were seen on TV. Playing opponents, usually billed as the All-

Ann Calvello, center, a Hall of Fame veteran of more than twenty years of Derby warfare and a captain of women's squads, is among the most colorful of top feminine players, with a flair for theatrics and a whim for dyeing her hair blue, green, pink, or polka dot. At left is Bay Bomber star Margie Laszlo, and at right Lydia Clay of Midwest Pioneers.
Bay Promotions, Inc.

Stars, and traveling in a thirteen-car nonstop caravan, they carried their portable track with them in a semitrailer truck.

The track, with a Masonite-paneled surface for the plastic-wheeled skates, was made in sections like a huge dining room table with leaves that could be taken out to adjust its length. It could be put into a space two-thirds the size of a basketball court or normally be expanded to 105 feet around each side and 50 feet around each banked turn.

First job for the skaters when they hit town was to set up the track themselves in the recreation hall, college, or high school gym where the game was to be played. Afterward they dismantled it so it could be

Joan Weston, the "Golden Girl" of Roller Derby, an all-star great for a record eighteen consecutive seasons, is one of the nation's best-known women athletes because of her years at the front of TV screens. Long women's captain of the Bay Bombers, later of the Pioneers, she wears black pivot helmet (number 59), doubles as both a blocker and a scoring jammer. Below, "Joltin' Joanie" in action, eliminating some of her competition.

Jonathan Perry

trucked on ahead, while they got a night's sleep at a motel and then drove through the next day to some city as far as five hundred miles along the route. Between home games and tours they were on skates ten months a year, but the nomadic tours packed in spectators and sold from two to four million yearly tickets.

During the year the average Derby player put in some 2,500 miles skating around the banked tracks and traveled another 50,000 miles by car to and from games, which left little time for anything else. Skaters joked that the roundabout tours must have been planned in the home office by throwing darts at a map. One town got to look like another—skaters seldom took much interest in where they were or in seeing the sights as they traveled. Meals, often eaten at roadside stands, followed no athletic training diet and included a lot of hamburgers, French fries, hot dogs, and cokes.

Off the track, skaters spent their time soaking out aches with hot baths, catching up on laundry and needed sleep, playing cards, or watching TV. For most of the girls, hair-washing was a nightly chore, since the sweaty helmets they wore in games ruined attempts at hair-dos. When they dated, it usually was with opposite members of their teams, and tour romances sometimes led to teammate marriages.

Contrary to the public image of them as tough, loudmouthed battlers, many of the girls in private life were quiet, dainty, fastidiously feminine, with hobbies that ranged from knitting and needlework to writing poetry and collecting antiques. Like most of the male skaters, few women skaters had been outstanding athletes before coming to the Derby. Although they usually started with some skating ability, their skill was developed in Derby training schools and in actual play. For many of the Derby's recruits of both sexes, the sport offered an exciting escape from humdrum office, factory, or farm life, and popular recognition and big money for those who made it to the top. Some invested in real estate and in outside businesses to which they hoped to retire while still young. Despite the punishing nightly track battles and long road tours, most of them seemed to enjoy the life and were defensively proud of the Derby and their part in the sport.

Live appearances were a transplant of the taped TV action, with shrill timing horns, whistles, varicolored lights flashing as a clock ticked off seconds of play, and an announcer skilled at keeping excitement pitched high with a loudspeakered commentary that left nothing to imagination. So fans could follow the strategy at a glance, skaters' helmets were distinctively colored or striped to identify them as jammers, blockers, or pivot men. Top jammers could skate better than 30 miles an hour, but normally skaters moved in a five-stride: five

"Son of Roller Derby" was what some writers called the revived sport when it came back to Madison Square Garden again in 1970 and packed in a crowd of more than fifteen thousand Palm Sunday spectators.
Bay Promotions, Inc.

steps, coast, then five steps again. In home games, skill, skating ability, and competition were primary; on the road it was more an exhibition, with entertainment dominant.

As Roller Derby regained still another new life, new teams, training schools, and a league-like system of regional franchises evolved. Competitive teams played each other and road-toured within their own sections of the country, home-based in the East, South and Midwest. The new Derby also had its new stars.

Greatest male star was the Bombers' Charlie O'Connell, big in skill as well as size, repeatedly voted most valuable player, whose twenty-odd two hundred-game years of Derby skating had rolled him to fame and really big money. Joan Weston, blonde captain of the Bombers' girl squad, was the Derby's "Golden Girl," treated by her fans with movie-star adoration, deluged with fan mail and showered with gifts of flowers and candy. Her TV popularity was such that in some cities she had to disguise her appearance in public to avoid being recognized and fan-mobbed on the street. Ann Calvello's fans were captivated by her Derby-track theatrics, her flair for color contrasts in costume, and her whim for dyeing her hair a different color for every big game, from pearly blue to green, pink, and polka dot.

By 1964 Derby teams were playing more than five hundred games a year, taking in three million paid admissions, and taped games were shown on 110 TV stations. The next year, for the first time in a decade, championship play-offs returned to New York's Madison Square Garden after showings of Derby games over an independent TV station had gained a million viewers in the New York area alone. Among the spectators who packed the Garden, *The New York Times* reported, were many grandmothers and grandfathers with "fond remembrances of things past," some of them wearing old Derby fan club buttons from the late 1940s.

Two big ones in action—scoring champion Mike Gammon, left, a thirteen-year veteran of Derby games, is punishingly greeted by Cal Stephens, right, voted most valuable player of 1972 season.
Bay Promotions, Inc.

Sportswriters for a time still ignored the reborn Derby, but it hardly needed them. TV and live games had given it a sports world of its own, populated by devoted fans seldom interested in other sports. It appealed mainly to a blue-collar audience in an age of growing blue-collar affluence.

By 1970 the Roller Derby's return, dubbed by one news magazine "son of Roller Derby," was a recognized national sports phenomenon. Its millions of television viewers had boosted the taped games back into top ratings; a Palm Sunday live game at Madison Square Garden had set a then new single-game attendance record of 15,874; and newspapers, sports magazines, business journals, and other publications from the *New Yorker* to the *Rolling Stone* were giving it in-depth coverage. Books were being written about the Derby, and a full-length documentary movie, praised by film festival critics, started a whole Hollywood production cycle of popular movies with a Roller Derby theme.

Derby teams, crisscrossing some 60,000 miles of the United States for games in 1972, brought an overflow crowd of 18,881 into Madison Square Garden in April for a game in which the New York Chiefs, led by famed Charlie O'Connell, captured the International Roller Derby League title. That fall, at White Sox Park in Chicago, a game drew an all-time record of 50,118 paying fans who contributed some $179,000 to the box office.

Roller Derby definitely had come back, again, as big-time sport, stronger than ever in its latest reincarnation from the Thirties, Forties, Fifties, and Sixties. Or maybe it had never really been away.

Roller Derby comeback drew largest crowd in sport's history to White Sox
Park, Chicago, in fall of 1972; more than fifty thousand spectators.
Bay Promotions, Inc.

California-born craze for skateboards
spread across the country to reach a
frantic peak in 1965, when thousands
of dry-land imitators of seagoing
surfers took to stunting on
roller-skate surfboards, doing tricks
like the "totem" shown here.
United Press International

Skates
and Slats

Hundreds of thousands of young asphalt athletes, seeking the thrills of surfing on dry land, zoomed skateboards over America's streets and sidewalks in the early 1960s. The craze began in California, where ocean surfboard riders took to hitching roller-skate wheels to slats of wood and scooting them along paved walks near the beaches to practice their balancing stunts and aquatic skills out of water.

Surfers, experienced at piloting no-hands boards over the waves, adapted their seagoing knowledge to the pavements, and the fun spread inland to cities where there was a lot more pavement than sea. The wheeled boards transformed driveways, parking lots, and downhill streets into hard-topped imitations of the beaches of Waikiki.

The first skateboards were makeshift contraptions knocked together at home. Then neighborhood woodworking shops started to produce them. By 1963 factory-made models came on the market, and within a year the demand was so great some ninety manufacturers were turning out thousands of skateboards ranging in price from $1.98

up. Bigger companies jumped aboard the boom and promoted skateboards into a multimillion-dollar business and a national mania by 1965.

Beginners could buy simple wooden boards, about 2 feet long with tapered ends and with four skate wheels attached to the bottom, two at each end. But they were encouraged to trade up to more sophisticated "precision" boards, some of plastic or fiber glass, with double-action truck-wheeled mounts, nonslip wheels and other gadgets, priced as high as $50. There were also skateboard T-shirts available and special skateboarding shoes, although the great mass of sidewalk surfers shunned fancy equipment and opted for old clothes and sneakers.

It was mainly a sport of the young, from the grade school set to the college campus, but as it swept through the landlocked Midwest and on to the East Coast, more than a few adults were caught up in it. Whole families, toddlers to parents, skateboarded together; news photographers pictured skateboarding matrons, professors, priests, and business executives. A sidewalk surfing magazine attracted fifty thousand charter subscribers, handbooks were written, and songwriters got into the act to give the fad its own pop music. Theatrical stars, including Katharine Hepburn, tried surfing on wheels.

The sport also had its own instant stars, recognized "big wheels" who gained passing fame. Backed by manufacturers, some turned semiprofessional, acting as instructors, promoting contests, and displaying their skill to publicize skateboards. A national organization and local clubs were formed. Some enthusiasts talked hopefully of winning a place for skateboarding in the Olympic Games.

When reporters in a Minnesota town discovered that a boy had been traveling back and forth across town on daily mile-long trips to school on his board, they acclaimed him the champion of long-distance skateboarders. But he modestly shrugged off the honor by explaining, "I did it just because it was quicker than walking." Another eleven-year-old boy in Philadelphia became so expert he set up a spare-time skateboarding school in his home driveway that attracted neighborhood adults as well as younger beginners. His driveway training track was banked at the sides with sandpiles to cushion his students' spills.

On a more professional level, a big New York department store cleared a busy sales floor to install a run for waterless surfing demonstrations. In San Diego, although close to the real surf, two girls came up with practical reasons for preferring dry-land surfing. "Out of the

Skateboard riding produced many variations such as this not-too-successful attempt to use balloons as a sail. Picture was taken in Rome as the American craze spread to Europe, but by the end of 1965 it had already passed its peak at home.
United Press International

water, the fellows get a better look at you," one of them said, and the other added, "Besides, you don't get your hair wet."

Inspired by the wave-riding surfers, sidewalk imitators picked up their jargon as well as some of their techniques. Although skateboards could skim over the asphalt at 15 miles an hour on downhill stretches, speed was not the object. Balance, as in surfing, was the essence, with ability measured by skill and coordination in executing complicated maneuvers. Most expert skateboarding was done on a flat surface. Since there were no waves to propel him, the rider pushed with one foot until he gained enough momentum to roll through his surfing stunts. He steered the board by shifting weight from side to side.

A "kick turn" lifted the board's nose while it was piloted left or right, pivoting on its back wheels. A "kick out" was a downward push at the back that sent the board skittering into the air to be caught on the run. To do a "coffin" was to start in a standing position and wind up lying flat on the board with arms crossed. Skateboarders did head- and handstands while rolling, rode tandem for team balancing stunts, spun in circles. From moving boards they jumped over crossbars to come down again on their boards at the other side. When a sidewalk surfer took a spill, the pavement landing was a lot harder than into the water, but in surfing language it was still called a "wipeout."

Skateboarding also borrowed some stunts from skiing. There were "slalom races" on zigzag courses usually marked out with empty tin cans instead of the flagged gates of the ski slope. Other races were on boards that were "walked" uphill. Far from snowy mountains, low-level ski jumps were tried from outdoor stairways.

Nineteen sixty-five was the skateboard's biggest year. Spring brought a new outburst of the craze on Eastern college campuses. Freewheeling contests were held at Yale and M.I.T. At Princeton some seventy-five inland surfers held an informal tournament. An intercollegiate match brought together teams from Wesleyan, Amherst, and Williams on the Wesleyan campus at Middletown, Connecticut, where a competition in skateboard gymnastics was climaxed by a slalom race of screeching turns down a 60-foot cement walk. Williams was declared winner of the "Little Three Skateboard Championship."

Off campus in towns across the country, sidewalk surfing contests sprang up in parks, playgrounds, and supermarket parking lots. California, the skateboard's spiritual home, drew nearly a thousand top entrants from twenty-eight states to compete in the first National Skateboard Championships. Before crowds that filled Anaheim's ten thousand-seat La Palma Stadium for two days, contestants matched skills on two 100-foot concrete slabs that had been laid over the turf, trying for three top prizes of $500 scholarships.

But not all the land-bound surfers were skilled, and the boards were a risky thrill for many. As hot weather brought swarms of skateboarders careening into city streets, public alarm grew that the craze was becoming a menace to life, limb, and safety. Fans and manufacturers insisted the boards were safe when properly used, but on the chase for fun, hordes of small-fry ignored the dangers. A bumpy sidewalk or a manhole cover could up-end board and rider. Seldom had any sports fad produced more scrapes, bruises, banged heads, skinned knees, and some serious concussions and fractured arms and legs. One California woman tried her son's board and got going too fast. She landed on both elbows and soon had one arm in a sling and the other in a cast, but her son boasted that he had been using the board for three months and hadn't fallen off yet.

Boards skittered out of driveways into traffic, raced downhill through busy intersections, brought cars to brake-squealing stops. They collided with stone walls, trees, and pedestrians, bumped into shopping-center customers, chased strollers from paths in city parks. Some skateboarders took to night riding in the dark and to wheel-clattering early morning cruises when streets were comparatively empty but householders were trying to sleep.

Doctors at one hospital in suburban New York reported treating fifty skateboard victims in a month. At a California hospital twenty-two skateboarders with broken bones were brought in within two weeks. More tragically, several deaths were attributed to skateboard

Men, women, children, and even dogs took to skateboarding while the rage lasted—at least, this dog did. Named "Tiger," the year-old pup was introduced to the sport by his teen-aged owners in Portland, Oregon, who taught him to make regular downhill runs.
United Press International

accidents, two in New York and one in Philadelphia, from running into automobiles.

Medical associations warned of a growing number of injuries. An American Automobile Association spokesman said clubs throughout the country were reporting skateboard bang-ups. The National Safety Council was convinced that skateboards "constitute a hazard unless the rider exercises considerable caution."

Harassed public officials began searching the lawbooks for ways to protect citizens from the wheeled invasion and the skateboarders from themselves. Old laws banning roller skates and "coaster toy vehicles" were resurrected, and new ordinances were passed. Police in communities from California and Utah to Wisconsin, New York, New Jersey, Florida, and points between began a crackdown.

Some places restricted skateboards to closed-off streets and designated supervised areas. In others, police confiscated skateboards as a "public nuisance," impounded them for "obstructing traffic," or removed the wheels before returning boards to parents with an official warning. One or two towns were more severe, threatening fines and jail sentences if necessary to chase the boards and riders from public thoroughfares.

The craze started to die, partly from the public backlash, but more because the fad had lost its novelty. As interest faded, the sidewalk-surfers-for-a-season turned to newer things. Skateboards survived, but never again with the antic popularity of 1965.

CHAPTER 5

Floating on Air —Two Ways

Skiing over the clouds like a bird, this Delta kite flier at Cypress Gardens, Florida, soars free to float back to a landing on the lake from which he was lifted by a speed boat towing him on water skis. Unlike such towed water kiters, most land-based sky surfers launch themselves with hang-gliders from beach-front cliffs or by running down hills and sand dunes.
Florida Cypress Gardens, Inc.

Kitebirds

Hundreds of Americans took to flying kites in the early 1970s—not little kites on strings but big gliderlike kites balanced on their shoulders that they could ride beneath—to hang dangling from them like human kite tails as they were carried into the air. What had started in California as a craze among small groups of hang-glider enthusiasts had spread across the country as the fast-growing sport of sky surfing. On almost any weekend there were men and women hurling themselves from windy sea cliffs, desert rocks, and hilly ridges, leaping down sand dunes and grassy slopes, clinging to the kites that gave them wings to fly.

They were mostly young, but some were in their sixties, seeking a thrill the conventional airplane never gave: the fulfillment of man's ancient dream to soar into the air like a bird in motorless and unconfined personal flight. Their one-man and mainly foot-launched gliders seldom weighed as much as fifty pounds, could be carried on car tops and easily assembled, requiring no expert aeronautical skill. At heights near the earth's surface, using sea breezes and gentle prevailing winds for the lift, the modern birdmen skimmed hillsides and beach dunes, perhaps for only seconds but with the feeling of flying free.

The sport had reached into the past to revive hang-gliders that led to the development of the airplane and were all but abandoned for it after the Wright brothers put an engine to flying at Kitty Hawk. With an even longer reach back into history, sky surfers and manned kite fliers were recapturing again a dream of human bird flight as old as man's first wishes.

Chinese legend of 2200 B.C. tells of an Emperor Shun who escaped captivity by donning "the work clothes of a bird." For the ancient Greeks there was the myth of Icarus who conquered the air on wings made by Daedalus, until he soared too near the sun, melted the wax that held his wings, and fell to death in the sea. Artist Leonardo da Vinci, in the early sixteenth century, also imagined manned kites based on observing the flight of birds.

Mythical pioneer of sky surfers and manned kite fliers, Icarus of ancient Greek legend flew too close to the sun and melted the wax that fastened his wings.
N. Y. Public Library Picture Collection

Britain experimented with manned "war kite" in 1902 to demonstrate use for lifting a military observer above the battlefield to spot enemy action. Artist's sketch shows kite tethered to line-winding apparatus. Inset photo is of kite on the ground, ready for ascent.
N. Y. Public Library Picture Collection

Using kites to lift men and then fly them became reality in the late nineteenth century. Demonstrations by Captain B.F.S. Baden-Powell, brother of the founder of the Boy Scouts, led to British use of trains of big hexagonal kites to carry military spotters high over the fighting front during the Boer War. There were many other private and military experiments. But the "father" of the hang-glider and indirectly of modern sky surfing was German aeronautical pioneer Otto Lilienthal.

A manufacturer of machinery by trade, Lilienthal devoted his spare time to flight, an ambition from his early boyhood in Germany, where he was born in 1848. His study of birds in relation to human flying and his practical proof that gliders could be regularly flown became basic to aeronautics and led to man's conquest of the air. He was in his forties when he laboriously built an artificial 50-foot hill near his home by carting in the dirt and piling it up, and foot-launched his first glider. Like latter-day sky surfers, Lilienthal hung to his big-framed kite by his arms and controlled it by the movements of his body.

With that and various other gliders, some bat-winged and double-decked, he leaped from man-made hills and nearby natural hillsides hundreds of times, making some fairly long glides during more than two thousand successful hang-glider flights before he was fatally injured in 1896 in a glider crash near Rhinow. His hang-gliding, excellently photographed and widely publicized, directly inspired other aviation pioneers.

89

At left is Otto Lilienthal, aeronautical pioneer, whose birthday is
commemorated each year by modern sky surfers in honor of his
hang-gliding flights in the 1890s that helped man conquer the air. At right
he lands one of his bat-wing double-deck gliders after a foot-launched
flight from his man-made "mountain."
N. Y. Public Library Picture Collection

England's Percy Pilcher improved somewhat on Lilienthal's
gliders, but after several hundred safe glides was thrown over by a
sudden gust of wind and killed in 1899. In America, Chicago engineer
Octave Chanute developed biplane gliders and made more than a
thousand flights without accident. Wilbur and Orville Wright also
experimented with kites and towed gliders before producing their
successful engine-powered flying machine in 1903.

In the early days of powered flight, there was still much talk of
man's dream of being able to fly like a bird, to take off and soar into the
air when and as he pleased, perhaps with an engine-driven set of
personal wings. But in the rush toward the new airplane, man again
became boxed-in, confined to a piloted machine, not individual wings.

Gliding as a sport turned to soaring in what amounted to airplanes
without engines, and the hang-glider was pretty much put aside as
something relegated to the past. Here and there some scientists and
sportsmen were still interested. Hang-glider meets and contests were
held in Germany in the 1920s, and a few Americans kept the sport
barely alive. Manned boxlike kites towed by cars and motorboats
appeared in Florida and elsewhere in the 1940s, but were too clumsy
and expensive to gain real popularity.

What opened the way for modern sky surfing was the flexible-wing Delta kite glider. It was developed by NASA scientist Dr. Francis Rogallo as part of a government research project into military and Space Age use of man-carrying gliders. Its design was such that almost anyone could build one and fly. Triangular in shape like the Greek letter Delta, with a flexible wing of fabric attached to three ribs joined in an apex at the nose, these gliders became relatively simple and cheap to construct, easy to carry and store. By the mid-1960s some modified Rogallo-type gliders were being put together at home by do-it-yourselfers, with plastic sheeting and frames made of bamboo carpet poles, for less than $10.

The sport took off from there. Plans, kits, and manufactured gliders were soon available. For safety and more durable construction, aluminum tubing usually was used for the poles to which the wing was attached. Dacron and coated nylon generally were found to be better wing materials than plastic. Kitelike gliders of more complicated shapes and designs developed, but the majority were simple ones based on Rogallo design. Beneath the wing there was a frame or bar to hold and some sort of harness or sling, its style depending on whether the flier hung toes down or pulled up in flight to lie prone.

As the craze caught on, Southern California's shores were dotted with dozens of hang-glider enthusiasts, jumping into the wild blue strapped beneath blossoming fabric wings. Above the sandy beaches, Rogallo-type gliders were parked airport fashion, nosed into the wind. Television and the press gave much publicity to a meet near Newport Beach, California, in May 1971, the first of what were to become annual gatherings to commemorate Otto Lilienthal's birthday.

Before long, one California glider association had eight hundred members, another club three hundred, and the rapidly growing sport spread eastward, picking up recruits wherever there were hills to fly from. From hundreds the sport's following was building to thousands. They were in Indiana, Michigan, Missouri. A Boston meet on a public golf course to observe Lilienthal's one hundred twenty-fifth birthday in 1973 brought gliders from all New England. By then there were magazines devoted to the sport, manufacturers and suppliers were proliferating, and cars appeared with bumper stickers urging: "Lift up your spirits. Try hang-gliding."

Manned Delta kites meanwhile had boosted interest in the separate but related sport of towed water-ski kite flying. At Cypress Gardens, Florida, flights with old-fashioned large flat-winged kites had been part of the water ski revues since the early 1960s. Then a professional glider expert, Australia's Bill Bennett, brought his Delta-

Combining water and air sports, the first National Delta Wing Kite Championships were held in 1972 at Cypress Gardens, Florida, to start what were to be annual contests. Manned kites are motorboat-towed to lift them into air, then released for free flight maneuvers and landing in buoy-marked target area.
Florida Cypress Gardens, Inc.

wing kite to Cypress. Behind a speeding motorboat, the towed water-skier could be lifted to a high altitude, then be released to fly freely back to earth.

Gaining quick popularity, the water-skiing sport brought the first National Delta Wing Kite Championship contest to Cypress Gardens in May 1972, sanctioned by the American Water Ski Association and drawing fliers from across the country to compete. Two days of qualifying jumps narrowed the field to twenty-five; another two days of competition left seven fliers for the final round. They were towed behind five hundred-foot lines, with scoring based on free-fall time, 90-degree turns, and ability to land on target. The target area on Lake Eloise was a 10-foot square of yellow buoys surrounding an inner bull's eye of red buoys in a 5-foot square.

Paul Solovskoy of Minneapolis led all three rounds and defeated the six other finalists to become first champion. But at Nice, France, during a demonstration of the tow-gliding sport not long afterward Solovskoy was killed in a glider crash. There was also another fatality during a tow-glider exhibition at Dulles Airport near Washington, D.C. But with some new safety precautions adopted, it was announced that the water-ski kite championships would continue annually at Cypress Gardens, with Florida state as well as national and world title meets to be held.

The land-based sky surfers, with their mass sport of foot-launched flights, are mostly self-propelled, not towed as water-ski kiters must be. They generally shun all forms of towing as too dangerous for simple dry-ground flying. Safety is stressed, especially for the beginner, with care urged in the choice of a sturdy, dependable glider and in testing his skill slowly from the ground up. Sky surfers claim that with normal caution the danger of serious accidents in low-level flying is slight. They have a saying: "Never fly higher than you care to fall."

For the average sky surfer, flight usually begins with finding a sand dune or small hill about 50 feet high, with a gentle shallow slope and a steady breeze that doesn't exceed 10 miles an hour. After a pre-flight inspection to make sure everything is in order, and with the sail hanging loosely, he grabs the bar and lifts the kite until it rests on his shoulders. He makes a few trial runs on level ground to get a feel for the center of balance and the lifting power of the wing, then climbs partway up the slope. Strapped into the harness, he turns the kite into the wind that is coming directly up the slope, and makes sure his flight path is clear of people and other obstacles.

Grasping the uprights, he begins a fast foot-run down the slope,

In flight, skimming a sand bowl at Cape Cod, is aeronautical
engineer and hang-glider designer and manufacturer Michael
Markowski of Marlboro, Massachusetts. Markowski, who
edits and publishes a magazine devoted to the sport, was
among the first to bring the California-born
sky-surfing craze to the East Coast.
Skysurfer Publications

keeping the sail barely inflated until the speed builds up, then gently
pushes away from the bar until the sail fills and he is lifted off the
ground to fly. Once airborne, the flier controls the craft by shifting his
body left or right for turns, forward or back to climb or change speed.
A smooth backward push brings the nose up into a gentle low-altitude
stall for landing. With ground speed reduced to zero, he pulls his body
forward to land again on his feet. Between flights there is plenty of
exercise lugging the kite glider back up the hill for another try.

Sky surfers, looking to the future of the sport, think it may become
as popular as skiing, bringing not only club members together for
meets and competition, but family groups and individuals on vacation
holidays devoted to daily hang-gliding. Although ocean beaches still
provide the best flying sites, manned kite fliers in New England
already have taken to grassy ski slopes out of season. The time may
soon come, some believe, when snowless ski resorts are crowded in
summer months with humans soaring like birds.

The World
Championship
Inner Tube Race

Two things that are still free, air and water, are basic ingredients for a mixture of sports fun that has produced what may well be the biggest little annual water racing event in the country in terms of mass competition. The air is pumped into hundreds of automobile inner tubes, and the water is the Colorado River at Yuma, Arizona, where they are put afloat by some fifteen hundred racers in an eight-mile river run for the inner-tube racing championship of the world.

While thousands watch, the inner tubers all but choke the river with splashing humanity, racing singly, in teams, and as whole families. Held on Independence Day weekend, when a temperature of 103 degrees is considered comparatively cool, the event began as a day of fun for local residents during the long hot summer. But as the number of contestants swelled into the hundreds, some were drawn from California, Nevada, New Mexico, Texas, and other points as distant as India and Okinawa.

What started in 1967 as a little race that brought out seventy-six competitors soon attracted news photographers, television cameras, and worldwide attention. Somewhat to the amazement of its sponsors, it grew into an affair that involves not only the Yuma County Chamber of Commerce, but a local Citizens Band Radio Association and the cooperation of the Federal Bureaus of Land Management and Reclamation.

Since the lower Colorado River is not always a raging torrent, much depends on the government's release of water from upriver dams for the annual inner-tube run. The Federal agencies also prepare launching sites, access roads to the river, and a system of routing the crowds over one-way roads to avoid traffic jams on the way to the take-off place.

Everybody seems to enjoy the joke that the racers are all headed for prison—the finish line being the Territorial Prison built in 1875 to house desperadoes of the Old West. As an added attraction there is a downriver parade of floats, including such entries as a whistle-tooting reproduction of an old side-wheel river steamer.

Rules of the World Championship Inner Tube Race permit only standard automobile tubes to be used. They can be no smaller than 13-inches and no larger than 16-inches, and officials recommend new ones since "old ones may crack or leak en route." Only one person can board each tube. Team or family-group contestants are not allowed to tie tubes together. Contestants are permitted, however, to tow along tube trailers with food and supplies without losing their competitive status.

Racers can hoist their colors by displaying small pennants, but rules strictly forbid the construction of any deck, superstructure, or false bottom, or the adding of anything else. Contestants "must float on the inner tube itself" and are not allowed to use "fins, paddles, sails, or any form of gear that contributes to forward propulsion other than that achieved by hands, feet, and river current."

Sunburn is a hazard of the sport. "Long hours of summer sun mixed with partial immersion in the water," race officials warn, "can produce serious burns." Most inner-tube racers wear a protective long-sleeved shirt, slacks rather than shorts, and a wide-brimmed hat and sneakers. The sneakers are needed for disembarking at the finish line and for emergency landings en route on the hot sand along the river. Muscle kinks, after hours aboard a tube, are another problem, and some contestants stop to get out and stretch their legs. So that everybody can be accounted for, dropouts are allowed to quit the race only at designated checkpoints.

Entries close the afternoon before race day, with contestants required to sign in by then. On the morning of the race, they get official

All alone, but not for long, Becki Contreras, Queen of the World Championship Inner Tube Race, prepares for a test run before the Colorado River is taken over by the swarm of inner tubers who join in the annual Yuma, Arizona, downriver run.
Paul Miller

entry numbers and an armband at the starting line, eight miles north of Yuma. At the finish line each contestant must declare his official number as his time for the run is clocked. There are eight categories, with first-, second-, and third-place trophies awarded for each, plus the "championship sweepstakes" award for the winner in any class with the best overall time. Minimum age for those who race alone is fourteen, with the singles' races divided by age groups up to seniors aged fifty or older.

Starting times are staggered from 7:30 through 9 A.M. Family groups are launched first, then teams, and finally the singles by age category. An official starter clocks each take-off from the starting-line rope, the race is monitored at checkpoints along the river, and the total lapsed time finally is clocked at the finish.

A family group must include only parents and their immediate children, each in a separate inner tube but holding hands as their tubes cross the finish line together. Those who enter as teams of from two to eight contestants, each aboard a separate tube, also must finish with hands joined. Youngsters from ten to sixteen can compete in family and team races, but there must be at least one adult in the group.

During the early years of the races, in 1967-68, the course was some eleven miles long, with the starting line near the Laguna Dam. It was changed several times, partly because of slack water caused by river dredging and to accommodate growing crowds of spectators and racers. Finally, the distance was shortened to eight miles. Those changes, and the fact that downriver speed varies greatly from year to year, depending on the amount of water released from the dam, have made all-time winning-speed records almost meaningless. Some years have produced winners timed at two hours or less; other years, under different conditions, the winner has been clocked at a little over three hours.

For the first time a team won the world championship sweepstakes in 1973, when Lawrence and Fern Shoppe brought their inner tubes down the Colorado across the finish line in 3 hours 14 minutes. That was two minutes slower than the championship time set the year before. For the great mass of inner tubers who make the run to the prison just for the sport of it, and with little hope of winning, the leisurely downriver drift may take five to eight hours.

CHAPTER 6

Hoopers
and Loopers

Freestyle hooping, with a continuous sequence of arm, leg, and body movements, scores the most points in championship contests, with no limit on the number of hoops used to create original routines.
Wham-O Mfg. Co.

You can do two things at the same time and do them well, like whirling one hoop over your head while hopping in and out of another that is in a perfect spin at your feet—at least this National Championship finalist did.
Wham-O Mfg. Co.

Hula Hooping is a sport usually played to music, with a live band or recordings to accompany contestants and help the rhythm of their twirling routines.
Wham-O Mfg. Co.

More than a million, not all as expert as this young hoop twirler, try out for the championships through annual contests in six hundred cities. Freestyle routine demonstrated here includes a skilled Knee Knocker with the lower hoop.
Wham-O Mfg. Co.

The Big
Hoopty-Do

Some stars of the sport are better at Knee Knockers than at Storks, or at doing Hops, Alley Oops, and Wrapping the Mummy. But whatever their scoring skills, the best of them, regional title-holders from across the country, meet tough competition battling in the finals of the national championships held ever summer in California. The victory they seek is with the Hula Hoop—that craze of the late 1950s. Once almost hulaed to death, the hoops have survived their frenzied past to remain a popular sport of young America.

Circus jugglers were spinning hoops on their arms and legs and around their waists for a century or more before hoop twirling got an independent start in Australia. In that land down under, previously best known for the boomerang, a schoolteacher whose name has been lost to history introduced bamboo hoops three feet in diameter for exercise in gym classes. Other Australian schools took up the exercise; kids started hip-swiveling hoops of their own outside school, and some stores began to sell the hoops. Their rise to popularity in Australia came to the attention of an American toy maker.

Late in the 1950s the Wham-O Manufacturing Company of California made some trial hoops of scrap materials, and a company official handed them out to youngsters in his neighborhood. The test run showed that young Californians, like the Aussies, thought the hoops were more fun than anything that had come along in years—and so did some parents who borrowed them to get into the act. Wham-O called them Hula Hoops because the movements suggested a hula dance, registered the name as a trademark, and put brightly colored inexpensive plastic hoops on the market.

Almost overnight, America went into a nationwide spin. Demand for the hoops soon had Wham-O turning them out at a rate of 20,000 a day, and that was only the start of the whirl that brought other manufacturers rushing into production of thousands and then millions of hoops under various names. Before long, there were some forty competitors making them. The novelty and low cost, and the fact that almost anybody could spin one, made almost everybody want to try. The craze reached its peak in mid-1958, and by the fall of the year an estimated 20 million hoops had been sold.

Toddlers, small-fry, teen-agers, mothers, fathers, and grandparents joined in the great hoopty-do. It spread from the playground to the university campus, from city sidewalks to beach resorts. The hoops took Hollywood by storm, with top stars of the movies and television helping to popularize them. News pictures showed champion boxers, ball players, golfers, judges, nuns, authors of best-selling books, beauty-contest winners—even trick dogs, trained elephants, and zoo monkeys—looping the hoops.

Psychologists offered a wide range of theories to explain the craze. Some suggested that the hoop represented a symbol of the family circle and a desire for security within it. Others thought young hoopers were showing rebellion against parents, although they didn't explain what parents who also hulaed the hoops were rebelling against. American newspapers generally took a tolerant editorial view of hooping, but the Soviet press sounded off against it as an example of decadent capitalist culture. East Germany, however, admitted the hoop behind the Iron Curtain, and so did Poland.

A Knoxville, Tennessee, girl set some kind of a record by spinning a hoop continuously for three hours. Then a ten-year-old Boston boy beat that by whirling for four hours, which amounted to more than 18,000 turns. Others not content with a single hoop claimed honors for spinning fourteen or more at the same time.

Novelty hoops, some with bells, whirring noisemakers, and other added attractions appeared. But by the end of 1958 the fad seemed to

Kids refused to give up their hoops, and after adults quit getting into the act, the wild hoop craze of the late 1950s grew into a continuing sport for the youngest of Americans. Shown is a group of present-day recruits at a playground recreation center where competitions for city, state, and regional championships begin.
Wham-O Mfg. Co.

be dying as rapidly as it had grown. The market had been saturated by overproduction, and the year of the national hoop craze was over.

But the Hula Hoop was far from dead. At schools, on playgrounds, and at recreation centers, as well as on home sidewalks, thousands of youngsters who had enjoyed the hoops refused to give them up. They had hooping all to themselves again after most adults had quit. If the hoop was no longer a craze, it remained a sport of the young, and as sport was rediscovered by new generations. Still simple and inexpensive, the sport developed basic techniques that became standards of competition.

More than a million boys and girls through the age of fifteen now take part in annual championships sponsored by the Wham-O Company and community recreation departments in some six hundred American cities. Judged on a point-scoring system for six standard events, they compete for city, state, and regional honors, with each regional winner getting an all-expense-paid trip to Hollywood with a parent, to try for the national title.

Even Frankenstein's monster can't shatter the poise of former National Hula Hoop Champion Marilou Jones. The Hollywood touch is part of the fun that surrounds the annual finals of hoop competition held on the film-making lot at Universal Studios.
Wham-O Mfg. Co.

In the city and state contests, each contestant is required to enter all six events. The first five are in fifteen-second rounds, with from one to six points scored for skill, poise, and gracefulness. Those events are: circling the knees with the hoop in Knee Knockers; standing with one foot off the ground while the hoop circles the other knee in Storks; hopping in and out of a spinning hoop in Hula Hops; spinning a hoop from the waist to the feet and back in Alley Oops; and Wrapping the Mummy, revolving the hoop from neck to knees and reverse.

The sixth event is freestyle competition, with a possible ten points to be scored in a one-minute round based on creative originality and smooth, controlled manipulation of the hoops. In freestyle, contestants can use as many hoops as they like, twirling them around various parts of the body and performing acrobatic tricks with them. Standard 30- to 40-inch hoops are used in all championship contests. The hoopers can kick off their shoes and perform barefooted if they choose, and are allowed to use floor mats but no other equipment.

With state winners finally narrowed to nine regional champions, the national title match each August at Universal Studios in Hollywood is a celebrity affair for the young hoopers. Surrounded by press and television interviewers, the regional champs receive their awards and trophies from TV and film stars and prominent public officials. Messages of congratulation come from the White House and from governors' mansions.

In the nationals, the semifinal competition allows up to two minutes for each contestant in a freestyle routine, with names drawn by lot so that three of the nine are matched in each round. The five highest scorers in the semifinal rounds are eligible to compete in the freestyle finals for the national championship and prizes that include a $1,000 savings bond for first place, $500 for second, and $250 for third.

Until 1970 all the national Hula Hoop champions were girls. Rickey Low of Portland, Oregon, then a thirteen-year-old eighth-grader, broke the spell. He first won the Oregon state contest in 1968, was state runner-up the following year, and in 1970 captured the national title from the girls with a routine of manipulating four hoops by foot and toe. After his victory the girls never again had the championships all their own way.

Some of the sport's standard competitive events, used for point-scoring in all city, state, and regional championship contests, include the Alley Oop, top, Hula Hop, center, and Wrap the Mummy, bottom.
Wham-O Mfg. Co.

For the Alley Oop, the hoop is started at the waist, lowered slowly to the knees, and given a speed-up to bring it back to the waist.

In a Hula Hop, the hooper stands on one foot, rotates the hoop around the ankle of the other foot with a slight kicking motion, and hops from one foot to the other to avoid the hoop as it circles around.

Wrapping the Mummy starts with a hoop around the neck, bringing it to the knees, and ends with speeding the spin to lift it back to the neck.

Reaching out for the Frisbees sailing to them are youngsters
involved in Chicago's "Operation Reach Out," a city program
that includes an annual demonstration of Frisbee fun.
Wham-O Mfg. Co.

The
Frisbee
Fling

Somewhere in the world, at any given moment of the day or night, there are Frisbees in flight. By daylight and moonlight, indoors and out, the plastic discs are flipped by the millions in a sport that has become a hundred sports—some organized and some played by rules made up as the players go along. Mainly a Frisbee is a thing to be played with as the player pleases.

The Frisbee reportedly got its first start at Yale after World War II. Throwing empty pie plates back and forth was a campus fad, and the tin plates the Yale undergrads used happened to come from a pie-making company in nearby Bridgeport that was called the Frisbie Bakery. When somebody stepped into the path of a spinning pie tin, he was warned to duck with the shout: "Frisbee!"

Tossing pie tins was a fad than didn't last long, but long enough to give the game its name, and it did spread for a time to other colleges and to youngsters who began playing it around home. Like almost all fads, it somehow got to California, where a Los Angeles building inspector, Fred Morrison, saw some kids playing it. Morrison came up

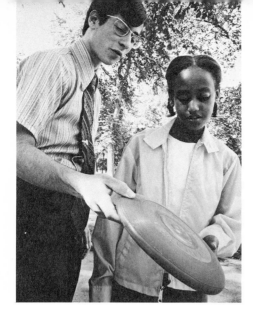

First a tin pie plate, then a Flying Saucer, it became the Frisbee— flipped by millions for the simple fun of spinning it into free flight—and an inspiration to invent new games.
Wham-O Mfg. Co.

with the idea in the early 1950s of making a play disc of plastic instead of pie tin.

He convinced officials of the Wham-O Manufacturing Company, which also gave the world the Hula Hoop, that the disc might become a profitable toy, and the idea eventually earned Morrison continuing royalties of close to a million dollars. It was first marketed as what was called a Pluto Platter, but that was just about the time the Hula Hoop was becoming a national craze and the Platter was more or less side-tracked as Wham-O's production and promotion went into the hoop. Later the disc was launched again, renamed the Wham-O Flying Saucer. Finally, with the ridge pattern patented and improvements made, it took off as the Frisbee.

Again it was on the college campus that the Frisbee, distant cousin to the tin pie plate of years before, came to first fame and found a lasting home. College groups across the country, discovering it mainly by themselves, started the fad that set everybody to flipping Frisbees. As Frisbees multiplied by the millions, they also grew into a variety of styles and sizes. There were mini Frisbees, regular, pro, and fire-orange sports models, the All-American, the Master, the speed-designed Fastback, and the Moonlighter, which glowed when exposed to bright light and became popular for Frisbee-sailing under the stars.

For many, the fun was in just throwing and catching the thing, watching it fly free, but techniques quickly developed. Backhand and underhand deliveries became the most popular, but there were sidearm throws, overhand wrist flips, thumb flips, curves, skip shots, and boomerangs. Simple one-handed catching added tricks like

108

Trying for a between-the-legs catch is this young contestant in New York state finals of the National Junior Frisbee Championships.
Wham-O Mfg. Co.

behind-the-back, between-the-legs, and one-finger catches. Accuracy, speed, and distance became goals of the expert. Frisbees were clocked in flight at speeds of up to 60 miles an hour, and could be sailed over level ground for 100 yards.

With creative enthusiasm, Frisbee flippers invented games that ran the gamut from simple spur-of-the-moment fun to skilled and tough competitive sports. The plain game of catch that could be played by two people almost anywhere remained basic. Trick shots and catches turned it into Follow the Leader. With a group of experts in a circle hot-dogging the Frisbee around, it was Sweet Georgia Brown. Keepaway made one player "it," while the others tried to keep the Frisbee out of his possession.

Frisbee was played across streets, from window to window of opposite buildings, on floating rafts, in swimming pools, and on obstacle courses where the discs had to be sailed across brooks or curved around trees. Frisbee Golf, with a course laid out to provide either nine or eighteen targets, grew popular, and there were Frisbee versions of basketball and lacrosse. There was Foot Frisbee, with throws

The Frisbee was brought to a new low by players who carried it to the floor of California's Death Valley. They established what they hoped would be an all-time low record by tossing their Frisbees at an elevation two hundred eighty-two feet below sea level.
Wham-O Mfg. Co.

Frisbee Golf, played over a course of either nine or eighteen targets spaced out like the holes of a golf course, usually includes water hazards and other obstacles. These students at Stetson University in De Land, Florida, proclaimed their first tournament as annual, traditional, and invitational, with the declaration at the bottom of the announcement that "Yankee ingenuity triumphs again."
Wham-O Mfg. Co.

and catches only with the bare toes, and play in which pet dogs were taught to catch or retrieve Frisbees.

Tournaments, contests, fly-ins, flings, and other Frisbee gatherings took place at hundreds of colleges, high schools, parks, recreation centers, resorts. Some of these events were planned; others just seemed to grow out of simple get-togethers of people who wanted to flip Frisbees. Annual college competitions ranged from intramural matches to team games between rival universities. Civic and community organizations as well as colleges sponsored Frisbee festivals, some of which attracted hundreds of contestants.

Frisbee marathons staged by fraternities and other groups, often as a means of raising money for some cause, tested the endurance of players and substitutes who kept Frisbees flying back and forth in continuous motion for days. A group of students at Millersville State College in Pennsylvania set a record of 217 hours, 45 minutes, 3 seconds, which was soon challenged by others in California, Connecticut, and elsewhere, some claiming records of 280 hours and more.

Frisbee flingers of all ages and both sexes wait for a turn at the action in one of the hundreds of meets that brings them together.
Wham-O Mfg. Co.

Meanwhile, for those who wanted tough team competition, Guts Frisbee grew into an international sport. Called that because it took "guts" to play, Guts Frisbee put two opposing five-man teams on firing lines only fifteen yards apart to sling the Frisbee at each other in a fury of fifty mile-an-hour speed throws, catches, crashes, falls, strategy, and zinging action.

Lined up behind foul lines across the fifteen-yard space, standing at arm's length apart, Guts players must make clean one-handed

Guts Frisbee requires not only intestinal fortitude but outstanding catching ability, as shown here by the Highland Avenue Aces during their win of the International Frisbee Tournament championship in 1972. Team captain Alan Blake, center, is making the grab, with John Connolly, left, and Tom Cleworth ready to move in if help is needed.
Wham-O Mfg. Co.

catches of the Frisbee hurled at them by the opposing team with the object of making the human targets miss the catch. One point is awarded to the throwing team for any legally delivered throw that is not properly caught. Trap catches against the body are counted a miss, but the Frisbee may strike one player and ricochet to another before the final catch.

Guts Frisbee had its start in 1958 when a group of young men on Michigan's Keweenaw Peninsula began a Fourth of July competition

Guts Frisbee champions demonstrate some of the plays of the game to a crowd at the Chicago Civic Center. Pictured are team captain Alan Blake, left, and John Connolly of the Highland Avenue Aces.
Wham-O Mfg. Co.

for vacationing families at the Lake Superior summer resort. For the first twelve years, the tournament was held at tiny Eagle Harbor, a village with a permanent year-round population of seven. It grew into the International Frisbee Tournament, drawing hundreds of competitors and thousands of spectators each year to the various places where it was held. As a game Guts Frisbee spread from Michigan across the country and around the world.

By 1968 the International Frisbee Tournament had become nationally recognized as the big event of the Frisbee world, as much a classic to Frisbee players as the Super Bowl or the World Series. Famed among its winning Guts Frisbee teams was the Foul Five, captained by George "Thor" Anderson of Gary, Indiana, which took the IFT title in 1970 by defeating the Highland Avenue Aces of Wilmette, Illinois. But the Aces captured the title in 1971 and successfully defended their championship again in 1972, in an overtime match against the Berkeley Frisbee Group Fuschia Team that was played at dawn, after darkness had halted the previous day's activity. Despite the early hour, more than five thousand spectators were on hand to watch the finals of a tournament that had brought some forty teams into play.

Frisbee was given another rapidly growing competitive game, with strong appeal as a spectator sport, when members of the

112

Columbia High School varsity Frisbee team in Maplewood, New Jersey, created Ultimate Frisbee in 1969. Roughly a Frisbee combination of basketball and football, with the Frisbee advanced toward the opponent's goal for one-point scores in passing plays but without bodily contact, it has carefully defined official rules.

Played on a 60-by-40-yard field by two seven-man teams, who may wear helmets, gloves, and cleated but not spiked shoes, it is a time-limit contest of forty-eight minutes divided into two halves. During each half, the players and the Frisbee are in almost perpetual motion. The clock is stopped for throw-offs (similar to kick-offs in football), for injuries, after goals are scored, for time-outs, and when the Frisbee goes out of bounds. The Frisbee must be played down the field by being thrown from player to player, not by running with it, while the defensive team tries to intercept or knock down passes. Guarding is permitted prior to a throw, but no contact, and a player may not knock a Frisbee from his opponent's hands.

Ultimate Frisbee, after being established in high school league play, made its intercollegiate debut in 1972 in a match between Rutgers and Princeton, on the grounds at New Brunswick, New Jersey, where the same two universities had introduced college football a hundred and three years before. Rutgers won the Frisbee game, 29 to 27, and also established another historic first by playing part of the game with a mixed team that included a girl, Peggy Delahanty, an

Frisbees sail by land and by sea wherever flingers gather—at meets, festivals, impromptu get-togethers, and at Frisbee frolics such as this one at Lake Tahoe, where a splash into the water to catch a high one is pictured.
Wham-O Mfg. Co.

attractive Cresskill, New Jersey, freshman. Mixed teams and all-girl teams already had played frequently in Guts Frisbee.

Frisbee is a sport with no governing or rules-making body, but the nearest thing to it is the International Frisbee Association. Started with only eighty members, the Association has become a worldwide organization of thousands of enthusiasts, ranging in age from ninety-year-old Frisbee flippers to newborn babes registered for membership at birth by their Frisbee-loving parents. The IFA, supported by Wham-O, the Frisbee's makers, publishes a newsletter of happenings in the Frisbee world, sanctions many tournaments, festivals, and contests, and has established standards of achievement for members who wish to test their Frisbee skills to be rated as amateurs, experts, or masters.

The first IFA Masters Qualification Meet, held in the Pasadena Rose Bowl, helped establish levels of proficiency for the various ratings. Under test conditions, officially scored and witnessed, qualifying members perform specified throws and catches for distance, accuracy, and ability to manipulate a Frisbee through flips, boomerangs, and tricks. Standards for a Master rating, deliberately kept high, have limited the roster of recognized IFA Masters of Frisbee to fewer than two hundred throughout the world.

Since 1969, one of the Association's most important activities has been the National Junior Frisbee Championships, which progress from local playgrounds to city, state, and regional run-offs, and bring together the top competitors from among some million and a half boys and girls through the age of fifteen.

The national finals, held in November, match ten regional champs in eight events: for flight accuracy in targeting a Frisbee through an upright hoop, delivery into a 12-foot circle, curve flights, skip flights, behind-the-back and between-the-legs catches, and distance flight. They produce some of the most exciting competition Frisbee has, with victory sometimes riding on one Frisbee catch that carries with it the championship and a thousand-dollar savings bond.

But the International Frisbee Association's philosophy is "Let us never take ourselves too seriously," and its Board of Governors is guided by the slogan that "He governs best who governs least." Instead of regulating Frisbee sports, the IFA is dedicated to the idea of allowing itself to be used by individual members and groups to serve their own purposes. It recognizes the fact that the Frisbee's basic appeal, however the spinning disc may have changed in form and substance, is still that of the tin pie plate—a symbol of each Frisbee user's freedom to use it as he will "to do his own thing."

REGIONAL U.S. CHAMPIONS COMPETING	POINTS AWARDED				I	II	III	IV	V	VI	VII	VIII	IX
	1	1	1	1	2	2	2	2	2	2	2	2	2
BRIGGS, Dick					1								
BRITTEN, Graham													
CHESLER, Don		1	1	1	2		2						
CLARKE, David		1	1										
GEMMELL, Steve	1	1											
LEWIS, Kevin		1	1	1	2	2							
McDANIEL, Mark		1	1										
OCHOA, Ezequiel	1	1				2 2	2 2						
SCHMIDLEIN, Kenneth	1	1	2		2 2	2 2							

2 Throws or Catches for each Event

ORDER OF EVENTS :

I.   Backhand Right Curve into Circle
II. Backhand Left Curve into Circle
III. Sidearm or Underhand (must be specified) – Right Curve into Circle
     Sidearm or Underhand (must be specified) – Left Curve into Circle
IV. Sidearm or Underhand into Circle
     Backhand Skip Flight into Circle

Scoring the championship play in the finals to decide the title winner of the National Junior Frisbee Championships: One of the finalists, below, is trying for a behind-the-back catch, while his competitors watch to see if he will make it.
Wham-O Mfg. Co.

Ancient Greeks were spinning yo-yos, although they didn't call them that, centuries before the craze first hit America. Illustrated is a reproduction of a Greek vase painting from the Berlin Museum, which is said to indicate that the string toy was popular at least as early as 700 B.C.
N.Y. Public Library Picture Collection

The English name for the thing was a "bandalore" in 1791 when the then Prince of Wales, later King George IV, was portrayed as a yo-yo spinner in this etching by James Gilray. The eighteenth-century drawing shows the Prince ignoring a royal scandal while idly toying with his bandalore.
N.Y. Public Library Picture Collection

By the time the yo-yo craze again struck England in the 1860s, to startle pedestrians in the London streets, the device was called a "sensation ball." Famed English caricaturist John Leech drew this cartoon for *Punch* in 1866 of "rude boys" demonstrating their skill as the rage became what was mockingly described as "the latest pleasantry in the streets."
N.Y. Public Library Picture Collection

Strings
on Their
Fingers

The yo-yo is one of those things that comes and goes, but never stays away. It has had many names. The ancient Greeks were crazy about yo-yo-like tops; so were seventeenth-century nobles in the royal courts of France and Spain. Napoleon's soldiers amused themselves between battles with a yo-yo known as *l'emigrette*, and by the time of the Revolution, the sport had so infected all of Paris that some prisoners reportedly yo-yoed through their last anxious hours while waiting for the guillotine.

In 1791 Britain's Prince of Wales, later King George IV, was portrayed in a satirical etching toying with a yo-yo when he should have been giving his attention to other things. Paintings of the period show various royal figures dangling the double-discs from strings tied to their gloved fingers. By mid-nineteenth century the yo-yo, called a "sensation ball," again had become a fad in Britain, where cartoons pictured London boys whirling them on the streets with an abandon that frightened pedestrians.

The United States has been captured by a repeating craze for the yo-yo that has peaked every ten or fifteen years since the first big outbreak in the late 1920s. But the American yo-yo claims historical descent not from Europe but from the Philippines. Years before Admiral Dewey took Manila in the Spanish-American War, which supposedly also led to American rediscovery of the yo-yo, Filipinos were using it as a primitive hunting weapon.

Fashioned from a sharp piece of flintlike rock, with a long thong tied to it, the come-back device was used by natives who hid in Philippine jungle treetops to conk small game that passed beneath. The hunter would spin it out and try to stun the animal. If he missed, at least he still had his weapon and could retrieve it for another try, without having to climb down out of his tree.

The yo-yo, which first swept America in the late 1920s and in repeated waves of popularity that reached a new high in the 1960s, once was flatter and thinner than it later became. Some earlier models, such as this, had an inner core of brass tubing around which the string was wrapped. Later yo-yos were all-wood and then plastic.
N.Y. Public Library Picture Collection

Over the years the yo-yo became something of a national sport in the Philippines, and almost every Filipino learned to play with considerable skill during childhood. Boys often spent hours carving their own yo-yos of wood, fashioning them with a precise balance for spinning and soaring. Some fine specimens, made from rare woods, have become museum pieces.

Typical of hundreds of contests that have filled the air with whirling yo-yos over the decades was this YMCA competition in Kansas City in 1954.
United Press International

The name "yo-yo" is said to mean "come-come," because that was what young Filipinos shouted as they spun them. Anyhow, that was what American toy maker Thomas Duncan called them when he promoted yo-yos to their first big popularity in the United States around 1929. As the craze spread across the country and then back to Europe to catch on again there, Duncan's small wood products factory in Wisconsin became the yo-yo capital of the world.

Other companies also made them, but Duncan's plant produced them by the millions and remained a family-owned enterprise devoted to the creation of the yo-yo until 1968. By then most of the competition had turned from wooden ones to plastic, and the rights and Yo-Yo trademark were taken over by the Flambeau Plastics Corporation. At Baraboo, Wisconsin, the name and tradition were carried on, and the company's Duncan Yo-Yo Division continued to make most of the nation's yo-yos.

There was a second big American craze for the yo-yo in the Thirties, another burst of popularity in the late Forties, and the biggest of all in the 1960s. Demand was so great that a dozen manufacturers couldn't keep up with it, and Duncan alone sold 15 million yo-yos in the single year of 1961. The spirit of play invaded homes, offices, and executive suites, produced policemen who twirled yo-yos when the flow of traffic was slow and postmen who yo-yoed while delivering the mail. Moppets, matrons, and men in wheelchairs, college students

119

Cradle play for expert young yo-yoers is this trick of "rocking the baby." Both hands are used to pull the string into a cradle in which the yo-yo is kept spinning back and forth. It looks easy, but has to be done quickly or the yo-yo will stop whirling. Beginners who try are likely to tie the string in knots— and their fingers as well.
United Press International

and high-rise building construction workers were looping, spinning, and "walking the dog." Plain yo-yos sold for from twenty-five cents to a dollar, but there were also silver-monogrammed executive models of hand-rubbed walnut priced at $8.50.

Meanwhile, the sport had developed a skill and dexterity that produced dozens of tricky plays and elaborate maneuvers. Deft turns of the wrist sent yo-yos circling into arcs, triangles, cloverleaf and star patterns, imitated the design of flags, spider webs, a Ferris Wheel, the Eiffel Tower. Experts could run a yo-yo through a cat's cradle; throw it so hard it would "sleep" motionless at the end of its string for seconds before whirling back to hand; flip it over the head, behind the back, and through the legs; and keep yo-yos soaring from each hand at the same time.

Records have been claimed, and some soon broken, for such feats as yo-yoing seventeen straight hours, or for looping twelve hundred consecutive loops. While there have been hundreds of competitions all over the world, most "champions" of the sport are self-proclaimed. Many are professionals who earn a full-time living from the yo-yo. They travel the country demonstrating their skill at schools, stores, and recreation centers, arranging contests, promoting sales, teaching. Some have been at it most of their lives. Others have turned what began as a hobby into an occupation. They are "champions" mainly because few can match their demonstrated ability.

CHAPTER 7

Creatures Large and Small

Upsetting years of tradition, twenty-five-year-old Carl
Huntington of Galena, Alaska, defeated the old-time
veterans of the World Championship Sled Dog Race at
Anchorage in 1973 by kicking his twelve-dog team to victory
in a furious stretch run. Huntington overtook seven-time
winner "Doc" Lombard of Wayland, Massachusetts, and
three-time former champion Gareth Wright of Fairbanks, to
come from behind and capture the world's title in the
three-day, seventy-five-mile race, covering the total distance
in 320 minutes 57 seconds.
Anchorage Daily Times

The
Mushers

The dogs are small but muscular and powerful, more than a dozen of them teamed and straining in harness at their tug lines, eager to run as the seconds are counted down for the start of the World's Championship Sled Dog Race at Anchorage, Alaska. Grasping the upright curved handlebar at the rear of the light sled, the musher gives the command. He seldom cries, "Mush!" More likely, he calls: "All right! Let's go!"

Instantly the lead dog, almost intelligent enough to read his mind, takes off, with the team following the lead out of the chute. Riding on the long runners at the back of the sled, the driver pedals along, kicking with one foot as they speed over the hard-packed snow. On slower stretches he may hop off to run beside the sled, and push if the going gets rough. Ahead are twenty-five miles of the first day's heat in the three-day, seventy-five-mile championship for a share of a $10,000 purse.

Every few minutes another team takes off from the starting line in the downtown heart of the city, to loop far out into the suburbs and back, in a race in which literally seconds count. Victory was won in 1973 by Carl Huntington of Galena, over all the miles in the three days of tough competition, by a margin of only 2 minutes 44 seconds.

For Anchorage the mid-February excitement is like Louisville at Kentucky Derby time—but colder. Thousands of cheering, chattering, parka-clad spectators jam the crowd barriers six deep on Fourth Avenue and string out shoulder to shoulder along the trail, braving chilled feet and frostbitten noses for a glimpse of the panting teams and their ice-crusted mushers.

The race climaxes a big ten-day winter carnival of other sports events, contests, and entertainment called the Anchorage Fur Rendezvous. It was started back in the years when an annual fur auction, still held, was more important than the dog championship has become. Frantic followers of the sport now all but take over the city during the run that brings champion teams and mushers from as far away as New England. Armchair enthusiasts cluster around every available TV set to watch and listen to team-by-team radio reports relayed from helicopters whirring overhead, while time tower crews with stopwatches keep track of each competitor.

Despite the considerable prizes in the big Alaskan races, such as those at Anchorage and Fairbanks, and in dozens of others along a December-to-April racing circuit that stretches across the United States and Canada, few of the drivers expect to break even financially. They are in it for the joy of racing, and some with an interest in breeding championship dogs. The seventy-year-old sport has boomed into rapidly growing new popularity in an age of jet-plane and moon-shot travel, with an appeal that harks back to the primitive excitement of pioneer days when vital dog-sled transportation was a struggle of men and dogs against nature.

Indians and Eskimos were dog sledding in the Far North long before the white man came. For generations sled dogs were their means of transport and for carrying game, usually with a few dogs singly fan-hitched to sleds made of hides and bones or fashioned tobogganlike of wood. Dog-sled racing was a native sport before the first Russians reached Alaska in their quest for furs and territory. It was the Russians who hitched their sled dogs one behind another to a central towline. Sledding later developed the gang hitch that was to be used in modern racing, with dogs paired in teams and a lead dog in front.

Through all the arduous years of Gold Rush and settlement, sled-dog teams were part of Alaska's history of hardship, endurance, and adventure. They hauled the freight, served for personal travel,

Champion of women sled-dog racers, Roxy Brooks of Fairbanks, Alaska; her years of competitive racing since childhood led to double victory by the time she was twenty-two. She captured the North American Championship at Fairbanks in 1972, after six years of trying, and the following year won the three-day, thirty-six-mile Women's World Championship at Anchorage.
Anchorage Daily Times

carried the mails, ran dramatic races for medical help and survival. And they also provided winter fun, informal races that grew out of the boasts and bets of trappers and gold seekers that one man's team was better than another's.

Alaska's first organized races began in Nome in 1908 with the All-Alaska Sweepstakes, a grueling, mind-breaking, body-punishing test of endurance more than speed, demanding the utmost of dogs and drivers. It was a 480-mile battle over near-wilderness terrain against freezing cold and blizzard winds, decided as much by the weather as by the stamina of the racers. The course followed a telephone line strung to camps and villages from Nome to the little mining community of Candle on the Kiwalik River 240 miles away, the halfway point where they turned for the struggle back.

Drivers trained for it from November to April, with hundred-mile runs to exercise their teams of ten to twenty dogs, waiting for a break in the weather to signal the starting date. When they finally took off, everything in Nome shut down for the race. Schools were closed, courts adjourned, businesses locked their doors, and people surged about the bannered streets proudly wearing the colors of their favorite teams. The prize money was small, but thousands of dollars in bets changed hands as messages were relayed over the phone line and race bulletins were posted day and night.

The mushers stopped only for food and rest, and little of that since they set their own time limits for stops at camps on the way. Dogs were body-blanketed, their eyes protected with dark cloth shields, and some had little flannel moccasins to cover their paws. At each rest place the dogs were rubbed with alcohol, fed, and bedded down before the driver considered his own needs. He often slept on a bare floor with his dogs. The Nome sweepstakes went on annually through 1916, setting the traditions and winter carnival spirit that surrounded other Alaskan races. As the sport spread to other places, courses were shortened to less punishing distances to put speed over endurance.

Over the years, with interest fading at times but strongly renewed after World War II, the races at Fairbanks and Anchorage gradually came to be the Alaskan big ones. Today, the North American Championship Sled Dog Races at Fairbanks in mid-March draw top teams into competition for high stakes, and the championship is run in three daily heats for a total of seventy miles. Although dog racing in Anchorage began in 1917 and went through several revivals, its modern races had their real start in 1946. As dog sledding grew into the most popular event of the annual Fur Rendezvous, what had been the Alaska Championship at Anchorage became the World Championship Sled Dog Race in 1960.

Long before that, the sport had crossed from its Alaskan homeland into Canada and the United States, with some races run as early as the 1920s, others even earlier. In recent years many of the old races have been revived, and new ones have bid for spots on the circuit.

An old one of the great tradition is run in Manitoba; Quebec in Eastern Canada has been a long-time center of dog-sled activity; and at Whitehorse in the Canadian Yukon, a jump-off place for the Klondike in Gold Rush days, the annual Sourdough Festival in February has three big days of racing on the frozen Yukon River. Among newer international events is the Canadian Dog Derby at Yellowknife in the Northwest Territories, a long, tough 150-mile marathon.

Dog-sled racing was imported to New England in 1924. Local, regional, and state championship races are run in Maine, Vermont, and New Hampshire. One of the most important contests on the whole

Canadian dog racing teams on the frozen Yukon River near
the finish of a day's fifteen-mile run during three-day race at
Whitehorse.
Yukon Information Services

circuit, big in prestige, is at Laconia, New Hampshire, where a World
Championship Dog Sled Derby in February attracts some forty teams
and more than 35,000 spectators for its three-day run in twenty-mile
heats.

From Idaho and other Rocky Mountain states to Ely, Minnesota,
where the All-American Championship races are held, the sport has
spread through most of the nineteen-state northern snowbelt. There
are dog racing clubs in snowless Florida and in California, where races
are run with wheeled sleds. Hundreds of smaller weekend races are
held by various dog breeding associations from Arizona to Virginia.

Some mushers travel the circuit from race to race, spending the
entire winter in competition, hoping at least to finish in the money
paid to those who place in the daily runs. There are a few races in
which all teams take off at once, as in a horse race, but most are run on
elapsed time. Teams are started at intervals and race against the clock
for the best total time to the finish. "Day money" is awarded for the
fastest heats each day, and a team that can average 12 m.p.h. or better
over a long distance usually has a good chance of being in the money.

127

Except for the big events, most races are made in runs of ten to twenty miles. For twenty miles, an hour and a half is fast. There are always stretches of slow going, occasional spills, and runaway teams, dogs, and harnesses that get tangled. Civilization has added the obstacles of stray cars and spectators on downtown streets, where the majority of races start and finish, and weather can be a problem. It seldom gets too cold for a race, but a sudden warm spell can mean slush and the need to truck in snow to cover urban asphalt. City noises also distract the dogs; so do strangers who call to them or attempt to pet them.

Active sled dogs are in no way house pets. They seldom see the inside of a house, but receive more care than some humans. They dine on special rations designed to give them strength and speed, and their condition is watched as closely as that of human pro athletes. Although a dog may live in a kennel with thirty to one hundred others, each gets individual attention. On the road they live in their own compartments aboard specially modified camper trucks.

The coming of the "iron dog," the snowmobile, has reduced the use of dog sleds for transportation in many parts of Alaska. But racing has brought an even greater demand for the breeding and training of good dogs and has increased their value, so that top dogs may cost from several hundred to several thousand dollars.

Sled dogs are of many breeds and mixtures, but mainly of Alaskan husky stock, with sharp-pricked ears, heavy coats, plumed tails, and often with the markings of the Siberian husky for which show breeders strive. A few mushers have run whole teams of purebred dogs, but most run a combination of breeds in teams chosen for speed and stamina, not for their beauty.

Teams are almost unmanageable if the dogs are not accustomed to each other and willing to accept their lead dog as chief. First in line, the lead dog generally is fairly small, intelligent, responsive to voiced commands, able to react quickly to changing trail conditions. Directly behind the leader are the swing dogs, then the pairs of team dogs, and finally the wheel dogs right in front of the sled and controlling the behavior of it. Wheel dogs frequently are somewhat larger and heavier than their teammates.

The musher's command over his team is by voice, with a "Come Gee!" for a right turn, "Come Haw!" for left, and a vocabulary of other spoken directions that often only the driver and his particular dogs understand. Veteran drivers say there's no chance of winning a race unless the musher and his lead dog think alike, and they admit that sometimes the dog's racing judgment is better than theirs.

Two dogs are sometimes used together as a double lead
instead of one lead dog, as shown in this picture of a race at
Whitehorse in Canada's Yukon.
Yukon Information Services

Like their teams, mushers come in all kinds and ages. The world
championship at Anchorage was won seven times in ten years, starting with his first victory in 1963, by veterinarian Dr. Roland Lombard
of Wayland, Massachusetts. A man in his sixties, veteran of years of
competition and title-winning in other sled-dog races, the famous
musher has spent full winters following his hobby over the circuit
from New England to Canada and Alaska.

His strongest competitor in the Anchorage championship battles,
four-time winner George Attla, Jr., is from the small Alaskan village of
Huslia, where winning races is a community effort that has produced
several champion mushers and many exceptional dogs. Attla appeared in his first race outside the Indian villages of the interior in
1958, when he came to Anchorage to win the big one with only twelve
dogs. He owned one of them, his lead dog. The rest were put up for him
by relatives and friends to make the winning team. Attla won again in
1962, and twice took the championship from Lombard, in 1968 and
1972. Both of them were beaten the following year—Lombard came in
third and Attla fourth—but still finished in the money.

129

Stricken with tuberculosis that affected his right leg, George Attla took up dog-sled racing as a teen-ager in his native Indian village of Huslia, running despite the fusion of bones in his knee, and developed a racing style all his own. The "Attla kick" helped him win his first world championship at Anchorage in 1958, and he captured the title again in 1962, 1968, and 1972. Famed as the "Huslia Hustler," Attla won or placed in scores of other races and trained dogs that won for many other mushers, including some of his rivals for the championship.

Anchorage Daily Times

Some of Anchorage's best sled-dog racers have come up through the ranks from years of racing as juniors. Each year the Junior Alaskan Sled Dog and Racing Association holds weekly races in Anchorage from December through January, for mushers from six to eighteen years of age. The youngest race one-dog sleds for a quarter of a mile; those at the top of the junior ranks run seven dogs over trails of up to a dozen miles under adult racing conditions and rules. Joee Redington, who began as a one-dog racer, graduated from the juniors to capture the world championship in 1966, and at least three other former juniors have placed second in the championships.

Barbara Parker, who carried off the Women's World Championship at Anchorage for three consecutive years, from 1962 to 1964, also got her start as a junior racer. The women's championship, which had its beginnings in 1953, brought the female mushers honor and glory during its first years, but little else. It was not as long or as lucrative as the men's races, and at first some "superior" males snickered at the whole idea.

But by 1973 the women had come a long way toward taking home a good share of prize money as well as respect for their competitive skill, with three days of championship racing for the women's title, twelve miles a day for a total of thirty-six miles. Liberation also had gained them the right to run in nearly all the formerly male-only races in Alaska, but under existing rules men were not allowed to run in the Women's World Championship. If that was discrimination in reverse, no males were heard to complain.

Dog-sled mushers of both sexes share an excitement in the sport that keeps many of them at it most of their lives. What is the lure? Veteran champion "Doc" Lombard once explained his addiction this way: "I'm always looking for that perfect day when the weather is just right, the snow is fast, the dogs are running in unison, and you move through the woods effortlessly, with only the rhythmic panting and the jangling of harnesses to hear."

For the dog sledders, those days are still found, in a sport that was born in another time before the roar of machines.

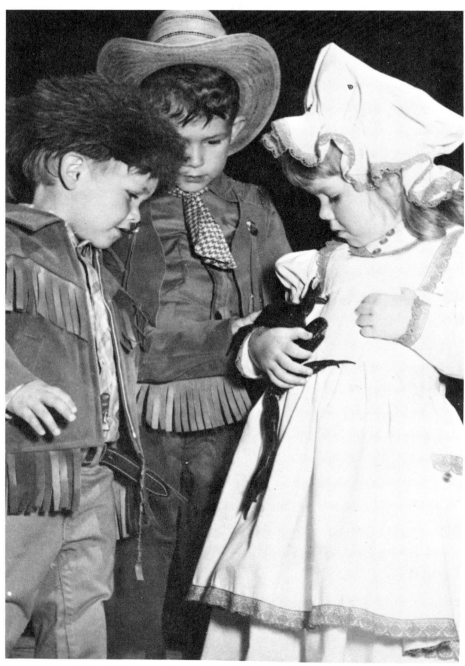

At the Calaveras County Jumping Frog Jubilee, where Mark
Twain's humorous folk tale comes alive again each year,
young Gayle Vineyard ponders her entry's chances of leaping
to victory in the special Kid's Day frog jump. Discussing frog
strategy with her are Danny and David Stikkers.
Hillcrest Studio

Jumping
Frog
Jubilee

"Now, if you're ready, set him alongside Dan'l, with his forepaws just even with Dan'l's, and I'll give the word." Then he says, *"One—two—three—git!"* and him and the feller touched up the frogs from behind and the new frog hopped off lively. . . .

When Samuel Clemens wrote about *The Celebrated Jumping Frog of Calaveras County* in the short story that was to help make his pen name of Mark Twain famous, he never imagined that his frogs would leap from the printed page to reality. As a newspaper writer who had done some gold prospecting himself, he came from San Francisco in 1865 to Calaveras County in California's wild Mother Lode country during the years of gold-seeking adventure. He lived for three months with pocket miner Jim Gillis and his partner Dick Stoker in a mountain cabin in Jackass Gulch near Angels Camp.

On one of his trips into the mining-camp town where he often played billiards and listened to the tall tales that were swapped, he heard a folk yarn about a jumping frog contest. Back in the time of the forty-niners, so the story went, a visiting stranger tricked the owner of a famed jumping frog by secretly pouring buckshot down the frog's throat so the frog couldn't jump and his own frog would win. From that Clemens created the story first called *Jim Smiley and His Jumping Frog*, in which he told how:

"He ketched a frog one day, and took him home, and said he cal'lated to educate him; and so he never done nothing for three months but set in his back yard and learn that frog to jump. And you bet you he *did* learn him, too. He'd give him a little punch behind, and the next minute you'd see that frog whirling in the air like a doughnut—see him turn one summerset, or maybe a couple, if he got a good start, and come down flat-footed and all right, like a cat. . . . And when it come to fair and square jumping on a dead level, he could get over more ground at one straddle than any animal of his breed you ever see . . . ."

First published late in 1865 in the New York *Saturday Press* and widely reprinted, the story of the jumping contest by the frog named "Dan'l Webster" set all America to laughing. As *The Celebrated Jumping Frog of Calaveras County*, it was the title piece of a collection of short stories that first firmly established Mark Twain's reputation. The leap from fictional folktale to living American folklore, acted out annually as a sports spectacle that draws thousands of spectators to watch the shouting, stomping competition for the frog jumping championship of the world, began some sixty years later.

In May 1928, after some struggle to catch up with changing times, the little community of Angels Camp managed to get its streets paved. With civic pride the citizens of Calaveras County decided to honor the occasion by holding a celebration. Somebody remembered that the frog jumping contest in Mark Twain's story supposedly had happened at Angels Camp, so for want of a better name they called the shindig a "Jumping Frog Jubilee."

When reporters asked if there would really be a frog-jump contest, the town boosters quickly organized one. Ropes tied to curb-parked trucks were stretched across the newly laid street pavement, a ring was marked off, and fifty-one freshly pond-caught frogs were entered. Five thousand people arrived to watch the whooping handlers jockey the frogs through their jumps. Women shrieked when some of the frogs leaped into the crowd, but the contest was a huge success. Mark Twain's story was permanently reborn.

The Jumping Frog Jubilee brought little Angels Camp worldwide fame. Through the years, combined later with the Calaveras County Fair, the grounds and buildings needed for the annual celebration grew into a $1,250,000 establishment. On the third weekend each May,

Frog jockeys, urging the croakers to jump, provide as much
action as the frogs. Once a frog is on the starting pad, its
handler is not allowed to touch it, but he can stomp, yell,
dance—or do anything else to get it to leap.
Hillcrest Studio

some seventy-five thousand spectators turn out for four days of fun
and frog jumping competition. More than three thousand frogs are
entered after preliminary contests throughout the United States and in
twenty foreign countries. Some jumping frogs have been flown in
eight thousand miles from New Zealand, others from Canada, Mexico,
South America, Europe,and Australia.

Governors of the states enter frogs for a special competition.
Others are backed by sports-world celebrities, movie and television
stars, civic clubs, and national organizations. Press photographers,

135

senior citizens, children, and other groups have frog-jump contests of their own during the Jubilee. Anyone can enter the preliminaries, and for those who don't bring frogs along there are rent-a-frogs available as well as "jockeys" on hand to jump them, for contestants who don't want to do their own frog-jockeying.

The wild antics of the jockeys as they urge their croakers on to victory with leaps, stomps, and yells provide action as unpredictable as the frogs. Once a frog is placed on the starting pad, rules forbid its handler to touch it, but he can do anything else to get it to jump—blow on it, flap his arms, yell, dance, throw himself into acrobatic stunts, or fall to his knees and plead with it.

A frog must measure at least 4-inches from stem to stern to be eligible and must be a true frog; no toads are allowed. Most of the jumpers are captured at night from ponds or streams, with bare hands or a net, after being momentarily blinded by flashlight. They are transported in containers padded with burlap sacking to prevent injury. The burlap is kept moist because water is essential to frogs, who don't drink it but do take it through their skin. Keeping them too long in captivity makes them dormant and less willing to jump; it also creates feeding problems, since frogs normally eat only things that move, like insects, minnows, and smaller frogs. But they can be force-fed small bits of hamburger.

The jumping pads are 20-by-20-foot carpeted tarpaulins. Since frogs jump only forward or to the side and not backward, they are started from a point about 6 feet from the rear of the tarp. Put in the center of a 12-inch starting circle, each frog is allowed three jumps—then the distance is measured in a straight line from the starting point to the point where the frog finally lands on the third jump.

The top-hatted, frock-coated judges carry canes. When the frog completes the last jump, a judge's cane is placed at the landing spot, and the straight-line distance from the start is tape-measured. Sideward distance is not counted. Each frog is allowed fifteen seconds for each of the three jumps and is disqualified if it doesn't jump in the allotted time.

Qualifying jumps are held until all frogs entered have been jumped. No contestant is allowed to enter or to jockey more than ten frogs each day. From the hundreds of frogs competing at the Jubilee, the field is narrowed down in the four days of competition to about twenty of the best jumpers. Winners of the preliminary jumps held throughout the United States also jump in the finals, as well as winners of the foreign competition. On the last day, the final jump-off decides the world's championship.

Almost overshadowed by pleading, the stubborn frog refusing
to leap beyond the shadow of this jockey's hands seems
unaware of the fact that an impersonator of Mark Twain is
urging the jump. The Mark Twain Look-Alike Contest is part
of the Jubilee fun. Frog jump judge, left, rests on the cane he
will put down to measure the distance—*if* the frog jumps.
Hillcrest Studio

A record to leap for was set in 1954, when Roy Weimer of Angels
Camp jockeyed his frog named "Lucky" to jumps of 16 feet 10 inches.
Ten years later, Bill Proctor and Leonard Hall of Lafayette, California,
set a new world's record when their "Rusty" jumped 17 feet 1½ inches.
Then in 1966 they broke their own record wtih "Ripple," who hopped,
skipped, and jumped a total of 19 feet 3⅛ inches. That remained for
years the all-time distance for any real descendant of Mark Twain's
imaginary celebrated jumping frog.

Volunteer jockeys hope to stay on and keep their "steeds"
headed in the right direction during the ten-day camel racing
season that is part of the Arabian pageantry at the National
Date Festival in California's commercial date-growing area.
National Date Festival

Capering
Camels and
Obstinate Ostriches

Camels, among the oldest of all domesticated animals, are never seen in a wild state, according to the experts—but you couldn't prove it by what happens when the starting gate goes up for them to race at Indio, California. Jockeys who ride the dromedaries during the ten-day camel racing season each February at Riverside County's National Date Festival claim camels can be as ornery as army mules. Few racing events are wilder or less predictable.

A camel may take off with a burst of speed and head straight down the track of the main arena. Then again, it may just stand at the starting gate, glassy-eyed, and not run at all without prodding and pleading. Once under way, the camels appear to enjoy the race, although they may shift directions and run the wrong way. They also seem to enjoy shucking off their jockeys and dumping them to the dirt. Not as gentle as they sometimes look when chewing their cuds, the hump-backed Indio steeds require careful handling.

Camel racing is unlikely to become a widespread American sport, even though the animal may have been a North American native that migrated to far lands ages ago. Imported camels were tried out as work animals in the desert country of the American Southwest before the Civil War, during attempts to establish an overland route from Texas to the Pacific. Later they were briefly used in Nevada's silver mines, but they scared horses, mules, and people, and there is no evidence that there was any organized camel racing in Nevada.

The annual races at Indio are a part of the Arabian pageantry of the National Date Festival in California's commercial date-growing area, to commemorate the fact that date palms originally came from Arabia and North Africa, also lands of the camel. During the ten-day celebration, camel races are run every afternoon—the camels supplied by an animal farm.

All jockeys are volunteers, mostly college students who race the often reluctant camels for the fun of it. Jockey lists are open to women on an equal basis with men, and to any spectator who wants to try. There are also races between clubs and visiting groups from other states. Camel racing draws big crowds but nobody stops laughing long enough to pay much attention to winning times or records. The object seems to be just to get to the finish line—and to stay aboard all the way.

Since ostriches, like camels, are found in lands that California's date trees originally came from, ostrich races have been added to the Date Festival's fun. Drivers, as in the camel races, are volunteers. They don't ride in saddles, but in sulkies pulled by the largest of all living birds.

Ostriches can run at great speeds but the Indio races are kept to a medium trot. While there is no truth to the notion that the big birds habitually hide their heads in the sand, they are likely to head in whatever direction they please. The jockeys use brooms to guide them, with a touch or a sweep of the air to indicate which way is straight ahead, but victory usually comes as a total surprise to the winner.

Sulky-riding ostrich race drivers use brooms, not to swat the
giant birds but to try to guide their direction and keep the
ostriches headed toward the finish line.
National Date Festival

CHAPTER **8**

Some Ancient Sports Revisited

This jouster is about to lance the tiny ring of steel that hangs from the ribbon above, during the Natural Chimneys Regional Park tournament at Mt. Solon, Virginia, believed to be the nation's oldest annual sporting event. Modern jousting has been going on here for more than one hundred fifty years.
Natural Chimneys Regional Park

Knights
of New

Older than organized baseball, older than the Kentucky Derby—the oldest continuously held sporting event of any kind in America is believed to be a jousting tournament at Mt. Solon, Virginia. For more than one hundred fifty years, since 1821, jousters have met there in annual competition.

Each third Saturday in August at what is now the Natural Chimneys Regional Park, against a background of natural rock formations that suggest medieval castles, they carry on the tradition, galloping their horses into action at the command: "Charge, Sir Knight!" But unlike the shield-carrying armored knights of old who lanced each other in deadly combat, they race against time to spear small metal rings with their lances in tests that combine riding skill with marksmanship.

One of the oldest of equestrian sports, jousting began in eleventh-century France and spread to England, where knights vied for honor and the favor of fair maidens by jousting each other bodily from horses at great tournaments of pomp and ceremony. Despite the casualties, jousting flourished as a popular sport of royalty well into the sixteenth century. Some of its traditions were brought to America by early settlers in colonial Virginia and Maryland. Riding and ringing games replaced the bodily combat of armored knights, but the mock ceremonies of "Ring Tournaments" preserved much of the pageantry of ancient jousting.

An adorned knight, equipped for jousting in fifteenth-century France, has capped both his own and his horse's head with doll-like replicas of the lady for whom he is about to risk his life in sporting battle. Colonial Americans, who imported some of the traditions of the sport, preserved the spirit if not all the trappings of pageantry, but substituted skilled marksmanship for the often deadly bodily combat.
N.Y. Public Library Picture Collection

For years American jousting remained a sport of the landed gentry, carried on by small private groups with the lists of "knighthood" restricted to horsemen of the "first families" in the tidewater states of the South. Contests became more public after the Civil War, when tournaments were held to raise church and civic funds and to build monuments to Confederate veterans. Gradually, and then quite suddenly in recent years as it grew in popularity, jousting became a sport open to all.

Women, never tolerated as riders in early tournaments, compete with men, and some children take it up at the age of nine. Whole families join in the jousts, as do city dwellers, suburbanites, and rural landowners. Almost entirely an amateur and noncommercial sport, its modern "knights" and "maidens" may be farmers, businessmen, housewives, career gals, or students in private life, when not charging down the field with lances.

Some of the bobbing lances they use are hundred-year-old antiques, others makeshift rake-handle spears tipped with television antenna rods as points. Steeds may be expensive thoroughbreds or plain nags, transported in motorized trailers or battered farm trucks. Shields have been discarded along with armor, except as fabricated costume in the pageantry before and after competition. Jousters wear ordinary riding clothes or even plainer jeans, but shirts are often emblazoned with chosen emblems of knighthood, and sashes tied to the waist proclaim knightly colors.

There are jousting tournaments in the West, Southwest, and elsewhere in the United States, even in New York City's public parks, but the sport's popularity still centers in Virginia, West Virginia, and Maryland. During the eastern season, from early spring until early fall, jousters travel a circuit of dozens of local, regional, statewide, and interstate events.

Maryland became the first state in the union with an officially recognized state sport after the Maryland Jousting Association, formed in 1950, helped standardize that state's tournament rules. In 1962 both houses of the state legislature adopted a bill, signed into law by then Governor J. Millard Tawes, to establish jousting as Maryland's state sport. Its championship jousts are held in Baltimore in early October. Virginia's jousters battle for their championship at the State Fair of Virginia in Richmond.

On the Washington Monument grounds, in a field behind the White House, some of the best of the country's jousters, as well as unknown contenders trying for the big chance, compete the first Sunday in October in the National Championship Jousting Tournament.

A rider races under the crossbar from which he has just
lanced a hanging metal ring during championship jousting
tournament at the State Fair of Virginia in Richmond.

State Fair of Virginia

Sponsored by the National Park Service, the Washington joust draws
a throng of spectators that often includes important international
visitors. Crowds are attracted as much by the costumed parade and
exhibitions of ancient jousting as by the championship competition.

Most jousting tournaments, wherever held, combine sport with
the fun of elaborate pageantry and tradition that attempts to revive
something of the age when knighthood was in flower. Knights and
maids enlist for the jousts under romantic names of mock heraldry.
There may be a "Knight of Three Birch Farm," a "Sir Knight of Cedar
Brook," a "Maid of Sleepy Glen." All female riders, whatever their
marital status, are "maids." Some jousters adopt more humorous
titles, such as, "Knight of the Night," "Sir Tight Knight," or "Maiden
U.S.A."

Gaily colored flags and pennants transform ordinary fields and
dirt tracks into medieval courts of tournament for a day. The presiding
official rules in kingly crown and robe from a royal grandstand,
although that may be only the flatbed of a truck bedecked with bunt-
ing. Youngsters are dressed as princesses and pages, and there are
trumpeting heralds, lavishly costumed "ladies-in-waiting," sometimes
a procession of knights to parade in artificial armor.

148

"Threading the needle" with skilled precision, a jouster captures one of the smaller rings on the tip of his lance. In some tournaments, rings are suspended from the center of full wooden arches rather than the portable take-apart bar shown here. Despite the modern conveniences, this jouster still sports his "knightly" colors on the doublet that tops his ordinary clothes.
tate Fair of Virginia

Some of the elaborate pomp and ceremony of
early jousting is shown in this reproduction of a
painting from Laxenburg Castle, Austria, of
knights on their way to a fifteenth-century
tournament. Pageantry is still part of the fun, but
modern jousters discard all the fancy trappings
during the real competition of the sport.
N.Y. Public Library Picture Collection

Festivities vary depending on the occasion, mood, and budget of
the sponsoring club. There may be exhibitions of jousting combat,
skits, and stunts featuring Sir Lancelot and King Arthur's Court, lions
and unicorns, the slaying of a dragon. Long tradition calls for an
inspirational speech from a guest of honor who addresses the assembled knights before the jousting begins, with flowery old-
fashioned oratory expected. His "charge to the knights" usually ends
with the words, "Charge, gallant knights, fair eyes look upon your
deeds!"

150

But most of the trappings are discarded when the serious competition starts. The modernized ancient sport requires sophisticated skill, balance, precision, and expert riding that comes from pounding hours of practice and training. Modern jousters, tilting lances at tiny rings of steel, have no big human-sized targets. Their civilized jousting is less dangerous than bodily combat, but it demands more ability.

Carefully balancing his steel-tipped lance, which is about 7 feet long and weighs about a pound, each rider waits his turn for the command to charge. He takes off at a gallop on an 80-yard run along a straight course down a track beneath three overhead arches. The arches are spaced out, 20 yards, 30 yards, and another 30 yards apart.

A modern knight answers the charge,
with only nine seconds to gallop the
distance and lance the rings.
State Fair of Virginia

Dangling from each of them is a metal ring wrapped with white cord. He spears each ring as he rides, trying to get and carry away all three on the long tip of his lance, within a time limit of 9 seconds.

Rings that are 1¾ inches in diameter are used at the start. Each jouster gets three rides, trying for them. Those who lance the large ones then get one charge at smaller-size rings. If there are still ties, even smaller rings are used; the size is reduced after each run until rings ¼ inch in diameter are used. The competition goes on until only one rider remains, with all others eliminated, and the winning knight or maid is declared tournament champion.

Some expert jousters argue that a good horse is most of the battle, while others believe the secret is in training the hand to follow the eye. There are those who "ride in the stirrups," standing in the saddle as they charge down the track, and those who crouch forward and concentrate on "threading the needle."

However he wins, the champion knight is acclaimed with great ceremony. He not only collects his prize award but gets to name the lady of his choice as "Queen of Love and Beauty." Leading her across a red carpet to her throne, he crowns her with a floral wreath and claims a kiss as a pledge of love. But if a maid wins the joust, there is no "King of Love and Beauty." She gets to name the man of her choice to crown her as the queen to be kissed. Then the pageantry and feasting—even if only on hamburgers and hot dogs—goes on into the night.

152

Cowboy
Charioteers

Splice a Hollywood Western with scenes from *Ben Hur*, and the unlikely combination of cowboys and Roman chariots might reveal some of the spirit and action of modern chariot races. The ancient sport in modern style, thanks to Western horsemen, is having its greatest revival since the days of the Roman Empire.

Interest in chariot racing is spreading to California, Oklahoma, Ohio, and other parts of the United States, but the heart of the sport is in the Rocky Mountains, where it was reborn. There, from November through March, charioteers in Western garb put their horse teams and chariots through dozens of local and regional races, competing for a place in the annual world championships at Pocatello, Idaho.

Actually the glory that was Rome's came as sort of an afterthought to those who revived chariot racing. The sport got its new start from the Western traditions of men and horses. Back in the years when ranchers made winter trips into town with sleds pulled by teams of horses, there would be a race now and then to settle bets and friendly arguments. In several Idaho and Wyoming communities it

153

Modern charioteers in dirt-flying action combine the
horsemanship of Western ranchers with the traditions of
Rome in the fast-growing revival of ancient chariot races,
streamlined for speed.
Cutter and Chariot Racing World

grew into a somewhat regular wintertime sport in the 1930s, with a
town's main street turned into a race course for horse-drawn cutters
on snow runners.

Then speedier cattle ponies were introduced to replace draft and
workhorses. There were some horsemen who wanted to extend the
impromptu racing season beyond the months of ice and snow, and
sleds were traded for makeshift wheeled chariots so dirt track races
could be held. As more sportsmen became interested, chariot racing
spread from Idaho and Wyoming into parts of Utah, Colorado, and
Montana, but still in a generally informal way. Some clubs were
formed, but there were few standard rules for competition.

As the new charioteers became aware that they were reviving one
of the oldest of sports, there was a slow mix of Western horsemanship
with some of the traditions of ancient Rome. A bit of digging into
history books revealed principles of chariot construction that could be

Chariot races in Ancient Rome were deadly life-and-death struggles, with drivers often trapped in the tangled wreckage of crashed chariots or imprisoned by reins, then dragged and trampled. Modern charioteers, taking a lesson from history, changed the rules to substitute speed and sportsmanship. Four-horse teams, shown in the artist's conception of a Roman race in Caesar's time when charioteering was the biggest of ancient pro sports, have been replaced with modern two-horse teams.

N.Y. *Public Library Picture Collection*

adapted to modern chariots—and also some things about chariot racing in Roman times that nobody wanted to revive, mainly the fact that the old Roman races were designed to increase risks of injury and death.

It was danger, more than speed or sportsmanship, that packed crowds of 200,000 race-mad Romans into the Circus Maximus and filled half a dozen other racing arenas in the age of the emperors. Chariot racing was ancient Rome's big pro sport, tightly controlled by four rival racing syndicates known from their racing colors as the Reds, Whites, Blues, and Greens. The syndicates spent huge sums of money on horses, chariots, and the training and trading of star charioteers to stage team races under contract to wealthy sponsors. Top drivers, many of them poor men and former slaves who rose to fame and riches, were the great popular heroes of the day. Avidly devoted fans bet everything on the charioteers' ability to survive the life-and-death struggle of the race. The thrill was in gambling that a favorite would escape a chariot crash or be trampled to death in tangled wreckage.

Like latter-day football or hockey players, the Roman chariot drivers wore defensive armor of tight helmets, shoulder pads, and heavy leather leg protectors. But when they raced, the reins were knotted and tightly wrapped around their waists, binding the driver to the chariot and horses. He carried a knife at his belt to cut the reins so as not to be dragged to death if thrown, or to cut the traces if a horse fell and was entangled.

Tracks then were narrow, with short straight stretches, sharp turns, and a stone-pillared median, all crash-making obstacles to shatter a wooden chariot whose driver cut too close. Eight chariots or more, each drawn by two, four, or more horses, squeezed into the tracks at once. The Roman drivers were encouraged to turn their chariots against one another, to cut across the track and block chariots behind them, or to upset rival chariots if they could. Rules permitted the greatest possible rolling carnage so as to feed the excitement of thrill-hungry crowds.

Fans then hardly cared about speed records or accurate measurement of the distance. The average Roman race was seven laps, but arenas varied in size, which meant the running combat might go on for a total of three to five miles. Ancient chariots were heavy lumbering vehicles, and the horses ran unshod, slowed by the soft sand beds of the tracks. No attempt was made to time the runs. All that counted was winning, no matter how or how fast.

Today's charioteers of America's West, while proud of the heritage of their sport, have taken a lesson from history in writing rules that put speed and sportsmanship first. Deadly combat on wheels, and crowded narrow-curved tracks strewn with a wreckage of men and crashed chariots, have been replaced with fast straightaway dirt-flying action. Modern chariot racing has grown into an organized, well-regulated sport, with interest in more than thrills alone. There are still some accidents, but few serious injuries.

Some of the new chariot-racing enthusiasts got together in the early 1960s and formed the World's Champion Cutter and Chariot Racing Association. Formally organized in 1964, it sponsored its first championships the following year with entries from fourteen clubs. In less than ten years there were thirty affiliated chariot racing associations competing in races five months of the year, and new clubs were being added.

156

Exhibition chariot races in California have attracted crowds of 50,000 spectators, but the new old sport's steadiest activity has been in the mountain states, where weekly races under WCCCRA rules decide the regional and state championships. After traveling hundreds of miles battling other chariot teams, 120 entrants finally qualify to compete in the world championships held in March at the Bannock County Fairgrounds in Pocatello.

Weather seldom stops the charioteers. Montana's state championships were decided in 1972 during a blizzard that blanketed the track with 4 inches of snow. Many drivers are ranchers, farmers, horsemen, sheepmen, forest rangers, and others with hardy outdoor occupations, but they also include bankers, advertising executives, college administrators, mechanics, and storekeepers. Women's Lib has had its innings, too, putting a number of female drivers into chariots. Marta Lowe of Kuna, Idaho, in 1973 became the first woman ever to qualify a team for the world championships.

The racing is open to those of either sex over the age of eighteen. Since drivers ride in chariots instead of on horses as jockeys, age or weight are not problems. With sufficient training almost anyone can become a charioteer. All it takes to get started is a couple of spirited horses, a harness, and a chariot. Some pay as little as $100 each for their horses, fashion their own harnesses, and build their chariots out behind the barn.

But most of the horses that reach the championships are quarter horses. Pedigree has become important, with thousands of dollars spent for some teams. The sport attracts many chariot drivers who are as much interested in the bloodlines of horses as in racing them. Recognition by the American Quarter Horse Association has made Register of Merit points available for horses competing with chariots, so that owners and breeders can add to the value of their animals by stacking up chariot race victories.

The chariots themselves, when specially built at body shops, also can be expensive, and there are the added costs of related equipment, horse trailers, feeding and training horses, and traveling to contests. Yet the experience of the driver and the handling and conditioning of his team still count the most. Victory doesn't always go to the team with the greatest credits in pedigree books. The skill of the charioteer in tough competition means more than what horses are up front.

Unlike the five-mile races of ancient Rome on sharp-turned narrow tracks, modern chariots speed down a 440-yard straightaway. Risk of accident is reduced by the shortened course, by two-horse teams instead of the four or more horses Roman charioteers used, and by limiting the number of two-horse teams that race at one time to three, or at the most four. Drivers are held strictly to rules of good sportsmanship, and no team is allowed "to pass in front of another team's line of travel or to interfere in any way."

The burst of speed over a short distance means many races are won only by a nose—which has brought in the use of photo-finish equipment and electronic timers as well as special starting gates. In the early years of chariot racing's rebirth, starts were by "lap and tap." Teams lined up as best they could for the gallop, held down until they were more or less equal and a starting gun could be fired. Chariot meets boiled with complaints of unfairness and false starts.

Gates to accommodate chariot teams, with plywood fencing before and behind to funnel them into correct position and guide them to an even start, were designed by the owner of a Pocatello machine and rigging company. The first time they were tried in the championships, drivers who had never ridden out of a suddenly sprung gate behind charging horses felt as if a rug had been jerked from under them. Several drivers were thrown when horses took the first leap. But drivers soon added handles to their chariots so they could hang on, and the starting gates, modified through trial and error and made portable, were adopted by affiliated clubs.

Under the rules, the combined weight of chariot, harness, and driver must be at least 275 pounds. The rules were written with a long backward glance at the chariot crashes of Rome, to reduce the temptation to build flimsy chariots that might rip apart under stress. Without gear and driver aboard, the average chariot now weighs about 120 pounds. Some chariot builders have devoted considerable study to ancient chariots in an attempt to combine the experience of the ages with modern technology. Whether they are history buffs or not, charioteers seem to agree on two fundamental principles—today's streamlined chariots must be light and they must be strong and durable.

One great advantage moderns have over the old Romans is in their access to light and durable metals in place of heavy and easily shattered wood. The metal stands up to punishing bangs and jolts of competition, and the reduced weight permits increased speed. Chariot bodies usually are of steel-welded construction, with 20-gauge cold-roll steel plate as the basic material. This is shaped to resemble a 50-gallon oil drum vertically cut in half. Some charioteers who weld their own actually use old oil drums. Many chariots are mounted on motorcycle wheels. All running gear and attachments are designed for

Specially designed starting gates spring modern chariots into the four hundred forty-yard race with a burst of speed that threw some drivers out of their chariots when gates were first tried. The drivers added handles to the chariots and learned to hang on. Because modern races often are won only by a nose, photo finishes are common and electronic timers also are needed.

Cutter and Chariot Racing World

quick take-apart and assembly, so the chariots pack for easy transportation to the tracks.

Firmly prohibited by the modern rules is the old Roman custom that tied the driver to chariot and horses, often with fatal results. Today's drivers cannot knot and wrap reins around their waists or be "fastened or attached to the chariot in any manner." Rules also declare that any chariot used must have a wide enough opening in back to permit the driver to jump free.

Today's races offer no Roman road to riches for the charioteers. There is little money for the winners, but most of them are not in the sport for money. They can reclaim some of their expenses from gate receipts. Seventy percent of the gate money taken in from spectators during the five days of world championship racing at Pocatello is divided equally among participating teams. But what is really at stake are the championships. Five trophies are awarded to teams in each of four divisions, and there are special trophies for sportsmanship, horsemanship, and best-groomed team. The first division champion is world champion.

Each of the thirty affiliated clubs enters four teams for the championships. Three teams of top-bred quarter horses compete in each chariot gallop over the 440-yard distance. If the races are no longer the life-and-death struggles of ancient Rome, there is the new thrill of speed and sporting action for the spectators. And for the charioteers there is the challenge of trying to beat the world record time set in 1969 by the chariot team of "Little Town" and "Safety Bars" of 22.39 seconds.

CHAPTER 9

Just for Fun

International race of pancake-flipping housewives puts American and English skillet-bearers into a dash through the streets of two towns separated by the broad Atlantic. Above is a view of the racing in Olney, England, where it all began five centuries ago, below, the run in Liberal, Kansas, on the same day. Results compared by transatlantic phone decide the world's championship.
IPDL, Inc.

The
International
Pancake Race

Carefully balancing pancakes in the skillets thrust at arm's length before them, housewives race against time through the streets of a town in Kansas and another town in England in a pancake-flipping 415-yard dash to decide an international championship. Behind them are more than twenty years of friendly transatlantic competition and a tradition that stretches back five centuries.

Legend has it that pancake racing began because of the old English custom housewives had of using up cooking fats by baking pancakes on Shrove Tuesday before the start of Lenten fasting. Some five hundred years ago in the English town of Olney, one of the wives was so busy making pancakes she forgot what time it was until she heard the ringing of the church bell, calling the townspeople to be shriven of their sins. In her haste she burst out of her house still wearing her apron, and ran all the way to church with skillet and pancake still in hand, to become the world's first pancake runner.

Just for the fun of it, other housewives followed suit the next year, racing with skillets and pancakes to see who would reach the church steps first; eventually, Shrove Tuesday pancake racing became an annual contest in Olney. The winner traditionally got a kiss from the bell-ringing verger of the church as he pronounced the words, "The Peace of the Lord be always with you."

In 1950 the pancake race crossed the Atlantic to Liberal, Kansas, after R.J. Leete, then president of the city's Jaycees, read about the Olney event in a magazine and arranged for his civic club to sponsor an American version. Leete got in touch with the Vicar of Olney, the Reverend Ronald Collins, who was in charge of the English pancake run, and set up the first of what were to be yearly international competitions. In later years Olney's Vicar Collins made several visits to Liberal, and in 1969 representatives of the two communities ceremonially signed a document officially perpetuating the transatlantic races and limiting them to Liberal and Olney.

Pancakes on a pedestal are a monument to the more than two decades of fun that the international races have brought to Liberal, Kansas, proclaimed by the town marker as the "Pancake Hub of the Universe."
IPDL, Inc.

The International Pancake Race

As the event began to attract thousands of spectators, celebrities, the press, and TV cameras to Liberal, the whole town joined in turning it into a mammoth two-day spectacle organized as The International Pancake Day of Liberal, Inc. Liberal, which with a population of sixteen thousand is the largest city in southwest Kansas, also claims a measure of sports fame for the enthusiasm of its fans that won it recognition as the "Number One Baseball Town in America." But the pancake races have brought it greater glory as the "Pancake Hub of the Universe," as proclaimed on a town marker above a monument of three giant-size pancakes on a pedestal.

The celebration begins the Monday before Shrove Tuesday with a pancake-eating contest at the armory, checked by official counters, then a reception honoring visiting celebrities, and in the evening a beauty pageant to choose a "Miss Flipper" as Pancake Princess. Race

More than a ton of steel was used to construct the giant griddles for serving pancakes to hungry visitors at the mass Pancake Breakfast that is part of the annual two-day spectacle.
IPDL, Inc.

day starts with a huge Pancake Breakfast on Tuesday, with pancakes served hot off a ton of steel griddles to the swarm of hungry visitors. Children's pancake races are followed by the big event, the Official International Pancake Race, and by a mile-long parade of antique automobiles, floats, drill units, and marching bands, an air show, entertainment, and an amateur talent contest.

The pancake race is run according to Olney rules. In Liberal, as in the English town, the 415-yard course is laid out in the shape of an S. In Olney the women start at the village well and race over cobblestone streets, past thatched-roof cottages and the Old Bull Inn, to finish at the church. In Liberal the contest is run over brick and asphalt streets, from Sixth Street and Kansas Avenue to a finish line at Fourth Street and Lincoln Avenue.

The women of both towns make the runs in housedresses, aprons, and head scarves, the head coverings traditional because of the church service that follows the race in England. In each town the winner gets a victory skillet awarded by the Jaycees of Liberal and an inscribed prayer book from the Vicar of Olney. The winning town takes possession for a year of the traveling trophy, a pancake griddle engraved with the names of previous champions. Also still traditional is the winner's award of the Kiss of Peace, usually bestowed upon the Kansas victor by the British consul for the area.

Weather and "track" conditions in the two towns are checked by transatlantic phone calls. Both races start at 11:55 A.M. , but because of the international time difference, the run in Olney actually begins several hours before the one in Liberal. Immediately after the Kansas race the results are compared by phone to determine the winning town and the pancake-running champion of the world.

As a continuing link of friendship between the two communities on opposite sides of the Atlantic, the pancake race has some serious purpose in helping to promote international understanding, but its main purpose remains what it was at the start—just good sporting fun. To keep the competition strong, any three-time winner either in Olney or in Liberal is automatically retired to rest on her victory laurels, disqualified from further contests.

During the days before the big race, the women do their practice training on country roads and athletic fields, and by pancake-flipping their way over the streets around their homes. There is a lot more acrobatic flipping during pre-race demonstration runs for the benefit of press photographers and television units than when the real racing gets underway.

On four hundred fifteen-yard dash through the streets of
Liberal, wearing housedresses and aprons, contestants must
flip the pancakes in their skillets three times and reach the
finish line with the cakes still in the pans. Displaying tricky
skill with a skillet is Pat Clark, clocked as she crosses the
finish line to win the 1973 race in Liberal.
Terry Hoggatt, Southwest Daily Times

In the race itself the rules call for a pancake to be flipped only
three times: at the start, at midpoint on the course, and at the finish to
prove the runner still has the pancake in her skillet, Keeping the
pancake in the pan and not accidentally flipping it out during the dash
for speed is one of the skills the sport demands. A pancake dropped on
the run does not disqualify the racer, but she must retrieve it before
she can go on, and the time lost can cost victory.

During the more than twenty years since the international pancake races began, there has been a seesaw battle between Olney and
Liberal, with the championship changing hands almost from year to
year. Liberal did win three years in a row, 1954 to 1956, and Olney had
three consecutive championship years, 1967 to 1969. Average time for
the skillet-wielding race through the streets in both England and
America is little more than one minute.

Following in their mother's footsteps are possible future
pancake racing champions in the making. These attractive
young ladies are competing in the Children's Pancake Races
that are part of the annual International
Pancake Day events in Liberal.
Terry Hoggatt, Southwest Daily Times

An all-time international record of 59.1 seconds was set in 1970 by
Kathleen West of Liberal. Two years later she came close to her own
record again, but didn't break it, when she ran the distance to win in
59.5 seconds. That was still better than 10 seconds faster than Olney's
1972 winner, Ella Crouch.

Plink,
Plonk,
Pitty-Pat,
and Shronk

Skimming flat stones over the water so they skip and bounce is no kids' game for the two hundred players who step to the rocky mound of championship competition in the annual International Open Tournament of the Stone Skipping and Gerplunking Club of Mackinac Island, Michigan.

With a wide-swinging sidearm delivery, a player moves into a low crouch to hurl a 9-skip that holds the large crowd of spectators in breathless silence as his stone skims the blue-green water of Lake Huron. From the judges' stand, play-by-play reports go out over a beach-front telephone to thirty radio stations waiting for news bulletins. TV cameras tape the action, press services wire the results to newspapers around the world, and everybody joins in the spirit of mock solemnity that makes the whole tournament a deliberate satire of American sports events.

It is a put-on in the grand manner, acted out every Fourth of July weekend as a witty spoof of much of the pretentious nonsense that surrounds other sports tournaments. Both the officials and the stone-casting players insist, tongue in cheek, that they are carrying on the ancient traditions of what was once a gentlemanly sport of kings.

Scholarly research has produced a club history that traces the pastime to dim beginnings, when some ancestral caveman first skimmed a flat pebble to watch it skip over the water. More directly, the game comes from sixteenth-century England, where it was known as playing at "Ducks and Drakes," because the motion of skipping

About to cast her stone upon the waters, a contestant in the International Open Tournament checks her grip for a sidearm swing, hoping for plinks and pitty-pats and not a plonker. More than two hundred stone-skippers take part in the annual sports spoof at Mackinac Island, Michigan.
W.T. Rabe

stones on the water was like that of wild ducks in flight. When kings and princes played it, some of them reportedly skimmed gold coins on the water instead of stones, with royal disregard for the state of the treasury.

The *Oxford English Dictionary*, dating the use of the phrase to the year 1583, declares that to make Ducks and Drakes of something is to "throw away idly and carelessly; to handle recklessly, to squander," a definition the players of the Mackinac Island club refuse to accept.

With pride they point to the fact that the game brought the military term "ricochet" into first use in the English language, and that stone skipping had its scientific application in developing the hydroplane.

The game was popular among British settlers in colonial America, and there are some who claim George Washington may have been the country's first celebrated "shronker" when he allegedly threw a coin across the Potomac River and entirely missed the water. But it was the

Rocky shores of Mackinac Island provide plenty of ammunition for stone-skippers, but a good stone is still hard to find. Male contestant shown here appears to be following the advice of experts to "keep your eye on the horizon, not the stone." Enterprising youngsters earn pocket money selling cellophane-bag assortments of skipping stones, but most skippers prefer to find their own.
W.T. Rabe

Stone Skipping and Gerplunking Club that transformed the play into an organized sport, with codified rules, a championship tournament, and loosely affiliated clubs around the world that are chartered as "Boulders." Officials include not only a grand judge, field judges, a steward, and a provost marshal, but also an historian and a poet laureate. The Winter Rules Committee meets annually, not in winter, but in August.

Lake Superior State College of Sault Ste. Marie, Michigan, sponsors the Mackinac Island tournament through what is called the Unicorns Ltd. Conglomerate, which also backs such annual events as a hunt for the mythical unicorn, a Silent Record Week to promote the virtues of silence, a Lizzie Borden Liberation Day, Sherlock Holmes' Birthday, and the ceremonial burning of a snowman to commemorate the arrival of spring.

Championship play in the July stone-skip tournament is from a rocky beach staked out with pennants and banners, with spectators perched on docks, on rock piles, or in lounge chairs. Some contestants from distant places bring their own choice skip-stones from home. There is no lack of them on Mackinac Island, since the nine-mile shoreline is almost solid stones. But ideal skipping-stones are not found easily, and great care is taken in their selection. Experts look for smooth, flat, thin stones, not necessarily round, weighing about 7 ounces and up to 2 inches in size. During preliminary warm-ups there is also much talk about water conditions. Choppy waves make for a "sporty course," but records are set when the lake is calm and glassy-smooth.

Lake Huron was as "flat as a flounder" back in 1932, according to retired Navy Commander E.M. Tellefson, on the day he claimed the greatest throw in the history of the sport, the hurling of a 17-skip stone for an all-time record. His claim, accepted by sports records books, has never been challenged. The eighty-year-old champ never competed in any of the official open tournaments, on the grounds that the greatest pleasure in having the title was in not having to defend it. But as reigning champion and chief field judge, he has had the traditional honor of starting the play by issuing the call to contestants: "Let him who is without Frisbee cast the first stone!"

From midmorning until late afternoon, the several hundred contestants compete two or three at a time. Each player gets to throw six stones during a round and is allowed a total of six rounds. Scoring is by plinks, plonks, and other terms officially defined by the rules, with play recorded on scorecards by the judges. A player's best throw out of six counts as his score for each round.

A plink is a clean-cut skip. Pitty-pats are the small skips that come in rapid succession at the end of a series of plinks. A plomper is a stone that lands flat and sinks without skipping, and a plonker is one caught by a wave on the first plink and spun into a nose-dive for sudden death. Shronkers are stones that miss the water because of short or wild throws.

Judging can be difficult. The first four or five clean plinks are easy to count, but the pitty-pats afterward are hard to follow. Some players

172

cast from an upright position, some kneel, and some make a running throw with a momentum that carries them splashing knee-deep into the water. There are sidearm, underhand, and overhand pitches, but the two-step wind-up that ends in a low crouch seems preferred. Experts advise keeping the eye on the horizon, not on the stone, and aiming for a minimum altitude.

World's champion stone-skipper, Commander E.M. Tellefson hurled a seventeen-skip stone for the all-time record in 1932. Retired from active competition with his title unchallenged, he has admitted: "Lake Huron was as flat as a flounder that day. It was sheer luck— couldn't happen again."
W.T. Rabe

The tournament champion wins permanent possession of the Little David trophy—if he can carry it. Handsomely mounted on an inscribed slab of waterlogged driftwood, the trophy actually is a 75-pound hunk of plain rock. Some winners insist on accepting it and lugging it away with them; others take only the slab of wood and find some rock of their own to mount on it after they get home. The winner also gets a year's supply of fudge, mailed to him in monthly installments. After the first hour of play, a pound of fudge is awarded each time the day's best score is topped. Contestants receive official scrolls for framing, signed by the tournament marshal, certifying their scores.

Gerplunking was dropped from competition in 1968, but kept in the name of the Stone Skipping and Gerplunking Club of Mackinac Island for sentimental reasons. Officials decided that gerplunking—the tossing of big stones for distance throws so they land *gerplunk* in the water—was largely an unskilled game, unlike stone skipping. Besides, it was hard to score, and the judges complained about getting wet wading out to see where the gerplunked stones landed.

Battling to break a ten-skip tie in the last minutes of play during the 1972 tournament, Dave Paterson, front, and Don Detter, rear, fought to a draw as the whistle blew. They divided the championship and also the Little David trophy, a seventy-five-pound rock, which was split with a sledge by contest judge E.M. Tellefson, shown at judging table on dock, so that the two champs could share the award.
W.T. Rabe

Next to unchallenged champion Tellefson, the best all-time stone-skipping record was made during the 1969 Mackinac Open by Dr. George Keitt, a New York biology professor, who hurled a fifteen-skip stone on flat water to win the best of that year's 225 competing throws. Brian Cossell of Kokomo, Indiana, captured the title in 1970 with a 13-skipper, a record matched by the following year's winner, Rolf Anselm of Flint, Michigan, with a stone that achieved 7 plinkers and 6 pitty-pats.

Hardest fought of the annual championships was in 1972. With only thirty minutes of play left, Don Detter, a 225-pound right-hander from Union Lake, Michigan, hurled a low zinger on his fifth try that skipped for a 10. Then with only ten minutes to go, Dave Paterson, hailing from Birmingham, a Detroit suburb, matched Detter's throw with another 10-skipper. They battled it out shoulder to shoulder, but were unable to break the first-place tie as the whistle sounded the end of the tournament. The judges consulted, and after some deliberation Commander Tellefson grabbed a sledge and broke the Little David rock trophy in two and awarded half to each of them.

Choppy waters in 1973 prevented high-scoring play, and the Open was won with only a 9-skip by eighteen-year-old Glenn Loy, Jr., of Flint, Michigan, who took the title by beating his own father's 8-skip throw. Meanwhile, some long-time residents of Mackinac Island, in the spirit of the spoof, raised a protest that the stone-skippers were depleting the whole island by throwing it into the lake stone by stone. In answer, the club proposed a wade into the water for an organized throw of stones toward the island.

A compromise was reached, nothing was done, and the traditional Awards Banquet was held at the Grand Hotel, as it has been after every year's tournament. Also by tradition, the winners never attend the banquet to receive their awards, declaring that they would rather "pick up their stones and go home." The club officials dine alone and make their speeches to each other.

Index

Index

Illustrations are indicated by page numbers in italics.